Tent Revival
for Agnostics

By Matthew T. Taylor, Sr.

2004 International Torch Association
Paxton Literary Award

MAXIMILIAN PRESS PUBLISHERS and colophon
are registered trademarks of
Maximilian Press Publishing Company

Author Matthew T. Taylor, Sr.
Edited by Judith Lane Stovall

Cover Design by John Walker
Photography by Jack Milliner

Manufactured in the United States of America

10 9 8 7 6 5 4 3 2 1

ISBN: 1-930211-71-6

Paper used in this publication meets the minimum
requirements of ANSI/NISO Z39.48-1992 (1997)
(PERMANENCE OF PAPER)

 Maximilian Press Publishers
920 S. Battlefield Blvd., suite 100
Chesapeake, Virginia 23322
757-482-2273

CONTENTS

ACKNOWLEDGMENT

I thank the International Association of Torch Clubs, Inc. for being the first to provide an audience for the expression of my agnositic ideas.

www.Torch.org

AUTHOR'S INTRODUCTION

What is it all about? What is the purpose of life? I really haven't got the faintest idea. So why bother with a book? I've bothered, firstly, because I wanted to codify for myself what it is that I know and believe about ultimate issues after 50 years accumulation of life experiences. Frankly, not everybody thinks the way I do and they should. So, the second reason that I wrote this is to convince others to join me. You will notice that I said not everybody "thinks" the way I do. I don't really care much about what anybody believes, as long as they are thinking about it before they commit to a creed. It is the method of questioning and verifying the conventional wisdom about which I am concerned. I am recommending some rational skepticism as an antidote to the natural state of gullibility in which we often catch ourselves. I am not preaching the skepticism of the ancient idealists who believed that, "one can't know anything for certain." It is self defeating to say that "one can't know anything for certain," and yet be certain about it. Got it? Good! Because life can be filled with certitude if we just exercise our ability to reason.

If you run with a crowd of philosophy lovers, or frequent the circles of religious scholastic groups, or have just been looking all your life, as I have, for the answers to questions concerning man's ultimate end, you've probably heard the arguments for and against the existence of god and will know that I'm not generating many new ideas. The inferences in this work are my own. For all that, I would never have been able to come to this point without the ground breaking efforts of the classical and contemporary philosophers and scientists who charted these unknown seas and forbidden routes in their own search for truth.

For the sake of the righteously offended, I would like to forewarn that the non-capitalization of the word "god" throughout this work is intentional. This is not out of spite, as some religionists automatically infer, but out of the logical consequence of my own personal conclusions that a definable god does not exist.

Therefore, I do not consider "god" a proper noun referring to an objective entity . . . at least, not at this point in time! After all, I am an agnostic and reserve the right to change my convictions upon any future discovery of new evidence to the contrary. Any revised opinions would be based on fact, of course! I do capitalize the names of religious groups, such as Christians, Jews and Muslims, because they do, indeed, exist.

I hope that you are inspired by the famous quotes at the beginning of each chapter. I have noticed the trend to add these types of quips in other works that I have read and felt it would be appropriate to do the same in mine.

I use the acronyms BCE (Before the Common Era) and CE (Common Era) instead of AD (Anno Domini) and BC (Before Christ) in designation of historical time references. I am not convinced that a literal Christ historically existed, and I consider this particular piece of "established" history a myth until I can feel justified in calling it a fact.

Tent Revival for Agnostics is scientifically and philosophically based. However, it is neither exhaustive, detailed nor beyond scholastic scrutiny. This is a simple treatise unencumbered with the empirical replication required in an authoritative work. The arguments made herein are brief for the sake of clarity, which can more easily be maintained through the compact continuity of basic inferences. Clarity, for non-scholars, such as myself, can be lost in droll details and prolonged citations. Proving beyond a reasonable doubt the assertions of my references is not within the scope and intent of this small book. Of course, the minutiae must be and have been gathered by my sources and the many other heroes and fathers of free thought, the scientists and philosophers who I am only, briefly, able to acknowledge. My desire is that you follow up after reading *Tent Revival*. Research the treatises of the brilliant exegetes who have done all of the foundation work. They have collected prodigious amounts of cites and sources for your personal confirmation of the facts.

This book is not meant to offend the many good people who love a god and are inspired by that notion to live in peace and harmony with their neighbors. *Tent Revival for Agnostics* should inspire them in their goal to know what god is, or isn't, in order to focus on the object of their quest. This work is an argument against the doctrinal theist as well as the assertive atheist. For agnostics, on the other hand, *Tent Revival* is by all means and in every sense a revelation and confirmation that they are not alone in their confusion and consternation over the myths that established cultures hold out as facts. *Tent Revival* will entertain folks of every opinion in that it is brief, logical and enlightening. *Tent Revival for Agnostics* can be read in one day or in one month. Enjoy!

IN GENERAL

The entire master plan is based on a lie.
Nietzsche

It is the damnedest thing, as much as I have journeyed in my life on the path for answers to the ultimate issues of life and death, even in a free society as the United States of America, that I never read the works of philosophical freethinkers such as Plato, Aristotle, Sir Francis Bacon, Descartes, Voltaire, Hume, Hobbes, Locke, Bentham, Mills, Russell, *et alia*, until I was in my late '40s. Marshaling the facts of life known to them in their time, they challenged superstitions and inspired others to use their experience and reason to improve their standard of living. In my youth I was introduced to Aristotle's syllogism during my studies as a cleric in a traditional Roman Catholic, anti-Vatican II, religious order, but its application was limited to the parameters of Thomas Aquinas' *Summa Theologica*. Under the influence of a religionist culture, I was prejudiced and put off reading the recognized works of authors such as d'Holbach, Paine, Darwin,

Nietzsche, Freud, Ingersoll, and Bradlaugh. Not one of these great thinkers, nor all combined, reached the knowledge of absolute truth. Nevertheless, they were brilliant explorers who overcame their immediate influences in order to brave the illegal and forbidden new world of objective thought. As a result they refuted a multitude of institutional fantasies and razed many an altar erected through superstition and ignorance.

Part One

Can I Get A Witness?

THE REASON FOR THE SILENCE

All great truths start out as blasphemy.
George Bernard Shaw

Most people, having been brought up within a religious doctrine, have a compulsive intellectual cut off to the argument of atheism/agnosticism. Out of psychological survival people mentally censor any public voice openly debating the existence of god. This opposition has always been virulent on both an individual and social scale. The consequences for publishing arguments against religious doctrine meant public execution in Europe before 1700. To publicize the premises for atheism was considered blasphemy in Europe and America in the early 1900's and a court conviction for the offense incurred certain jail time. The severity of censure of free thought has lightened up a little these days in countries where there exists a legal separation between church and state. In any event, intolerance to objectivity still exists within the religion instilled masses. A person may have legal freedom to speak on the subject, but the social consequences can be detrimental. I read on the internet (consider the source) that President Bush made the statement that he does not consider an atheist a citizen since, "this is supposed to be a nation under god."

Until declared unconstitutional in the early 20th century, many states forbade the testimony of atheists and prohibited them from bringing lawsuits to court. Their testimony was presumed to be non-credible. The exposed atheist could hardly be successful in today's political process where profession of faith is a platform for perceived moral integrity. What law-abiding, family-oriented, hard-working atheist/agnostic wants to stick his or her neck out in public by voicing a well-reasoned argument against the beliefs of an autonomic, well-connected, powerful religious filibuster? That poor person takes a high risk of being labeled immoral by a condescending "moral majority," many of whom may never even have heard of a syllogism or used a reasoned argument in their lives.

Speaking from my own experience, I can say that religious doctrine created within me a mental block which disabled any objective search for truth that I might have entertained while growing up. I remember sermons and literature condemning philosophy as the tool of the devil in deluding the faithful. The Bible says that god will destroy the wisdom of the wise and will bring to nothing the understanding of the prudent. That is a self-fulfilling prophesy in that religious organizations have been destroying the wisdom of the wise for centuries by burning them at the stake and obliterating their writings. I recall the Catholic Church's condemnation of atheism as the foulest state of depravity. I have read enough about the history of the inquisition to know that they actively backed up the premise with something that they didn't consider quite as foul: the torture and murder of its adherents.

Luckily, the pressures of religion let up during my pursuit of a secular college education. I have since read a multitude of works by atheists and Christian apologists alike. I have been persuaded by this experience and my own sense perceptions of several salient propositions. First, that mankind is fatally open to suggestion when it comes to its accepting answers to the unknown. Secondly, that the theory of cosmology and the definitions of omnipotence, omniscience and omnibenevolence, as applied to god, contain mutually exclusive terms in view of observed reality. Thirdly, the *Old and New Testaments* have authenticity problems and self contradicting passages which exclude the notion of infallibility.

THE LEARNING PROCESS

Uncursed by doubt our earliest creed we take;
We love the precepts for the teacher's sake.
Oliver Wendell Holmes, Sr.

Truth is not derived from authority.
Sir Francis Bacon

When we were children, the learning process took place through the imposition and memorization of information parleyed through the environment of our parents, teachers, churches and social authorities. As a part of our natural development and survival instincts, we are hardwired to acquiesce to authority. The trait of acquiescence saves our lives when we are young and inexperienced. Authority figures know and count on the state of acquiescence and use it frequently, for better or worse, to manipulate us.   The manipulation by authority in our early lives, more often than not, will have conditioned our responses to the predicaments we will face in the future.

Children accept information without question. The   wholesale belief and acceptance by children of the stories of Santa Claus, leprechauns and genies, relative to their culture, proves this. A child's credos are, for the most part, fashioned and accepted as infallible truths before its mind has comparisons and questions. Lacking the ability to assume otherwise, young sponges imbibe and retain as categorically true an unchecked flow of culture, doctrine and life style before the reasoning process develops. All concepts are categorical in the mind of a child. They take things literally. Their brains and emotional levels of experience are not developed enough to abstract the notions of grey areas, double meaning or sarcasm. This state of absolutism often carries on into late adolescence as the "idealistic" youth becomes the ardent follower of a creed, a cult, a political cause or the military. (Don't get me wrong. I am not criticizing a particular creed, cult, political cause or the military. What I am saying is that the absolutists like Timothy McViegh, Osama bin Laden and Jim Jones require and feed on the function of authority and structure.) I consider it such an unfortunate circumstance when I see older adults joining cults and radical causes. They have somehow not developed past the state of literalism and idealism that should have occurred in their youth. Life is too short to spend too much time in the idealistic phase.

Going back to infantile development, a child may be born with a genetic instinct to seek out ultimate issues, but a child is not born with a belief in a particular religious doctrine. A child is born an atheist with no belief in god whatsoever until its guardians instill the foundation of a particular creed.

A child is taught its religious doctrine through a process of passed-down-double-hearsay: one man said, that another man said, that god said to him, that this is what everybody should believe. Doctrines are usually instilled by a twofold method of relating the doctrine and then backing it with a threat of misfortune and punishment if not believed and practiced. Western religious doctrine wards off contrary belief with the indoctrination of fear of satanic control over the individual and the threat of eternal damnation. Eastern religion threatens ancestral punishment, terrestrial misery or a deprivation of karmic flow for the consequences of unbelief. Political doctrine is instilled with the threat of personal humiliation and loss of honor for the transgressor who becomes a traitor to the tribe or nation; and so on.

If the emotion of fear arises within you from an outsider's suggestion to read the critiques of biblical infallibility by Thomas Paine or Bertrand Russell, then the aforementioned point is made. If your anxiety level increases at the mention of names like Darwin, Marx, Freud, Nietzsche or Sartre, and you haven't even read their works, then acknowledge the existence within yourself of an occupying indoctrination. If you loathe to explore the various erudite arguments on the nature of god by philosophers like Hume, Hegel, Kant, Spinosa, and Kierkegaard, you are in danger of already having been hardened in the kiln of faith-based acceptance of reality. Scholarly works shouldn't harm the average adult

that can legally think and act for him or herself. Are people afraid of being led out of
their beliefs? They certainly are. And I will
get to that.

The agnostic, Robert Ingersoll, re-
minded us in the late 19th century that the
options of religious belief that nations or
communities will practice are like the
options of the clothes they will wear. The
particular styles, cut, and colors are
dependent on the culture of the country
itself.   The point is, and most observing
people will agree, that an Irish boy is
Catholic   because   his   parents   were
Catholic; an Israeli girl is Jewish because
her mother was Jewish; and an Amazonian
boy is a tree worshiper because his father
was a tree worshiper.[1]   There are, of
course, occasional exceptions of doctrinal
conversions which take place in lieu of this
generality.

We grow up in the psychological
security of these "truths" and remain content with them. As we age we develop the
ability to reason and, still wearing the rose-

colored glasses of our indoctrinations, rationalize our arguments for the ultimate answers relative to the knowledge of our upbringing. We become comfortable and indoctrinated as we achieve certitude and satisfaction through desultory comparisons and conclusions premised on this inbred, in-the-box, in house research. Consequently, within this environment we never really advance to the pursuit of knowledge.

That being said, it follows that a pursuit of knowledge relative only to our original points of view is generally not holistic enough for the acquisition of truth. The compulsion to persist in the original beliefs of our upbringing prevents us, through self censure, from acquiring outside knowledge requisite to making objective, *i.e.,* truthful, conclusions as to reality. Our perceptions most often remain relative and limited to the time, place and circumstance of our vantage point. The view must be frequently altered in order to think outside the cage of our original conditioning and grasp the bigger picture.

Outside information (that which opposes our own beliefs or comes from outside our culture) can come too little and too late to cure our psychological fixation on previously held beliefs. Whether credos and leaps of faith are true or false, coerced or learned freely, the longer we maintain them the more confident we are with them and the harder it is to convert from the comfort of our faith to the reality of reason. Without a victory over the compulsive resistance to explore opposing beliefs, we will never exchange our faith for objective reasoning no matter how untrue, unnatural, unobserved, unscientific or prejudicial to ourselves and others our beliefs may be.

AGNOSTICISM

Ignorance is preferable to error, and he is less remote from truth who believes nothing, than he who believes what is wrong.
Thomas Jefferson

The scientific methods introduced by Aristotle in the third century BCE and Sir Francis Bacon in the 17th century have had some time to bear fruit. Although the scientific method generally stays clear of metaphysics and ultimate issues, the business of accumulating evidence to support a proposition has disproved many theological doctrines and the creation creed. Religious texts have been dissected and analyzed to show their man-made incoherencies and chronological inconsistencies. The requirement of justification and the burden to prove religious beliefs has now shifted from the non-belieiver to the believer. As a result, the informed agnostic is ready and waiting for the opportunity to hear and question the reasons for any religious belief, but the onus to prove its worth is on the believer not the agnostic.

Agnosticism is a corollary to secular philosophy developed by 17th and 18th century French thinkers, Voltaire and Comte, and the English Hume, Hobbes, Bentham, Locke and Mill. Before it was given a name, it developed out of the structured arguments of these philosophers who, although they were theists, were raising doubts as to the rationality of contemporary religious and political doctrine. There were a few who attempted to publish this type of secular philosophy before the 16th century, but many of them and their works went up in smoke unless they published under pseudonyms and kept moving to avoid detection.

Born out of simplicity, the word "agnostic" was coined by Thomas Huxley, compatriot of Charles Darwin and a late 19th century philosopher and biologist. He combined the Greek prefix "a," which means "without," with the Greek noun "gnostic," meaning "understanding," to form the word "agnostic," *i.e.*, one who is "without understanding" or "does not know." An agnostic is one who does not know if god exists because there is not enough evidence to affirm or deny the reality. There are ambiguous definitions of agnosticism which are differentiated by slight variations. They include atheistic and theistic models.

I place the description of atheism into one of two categories. One is active and asserts a denial of the existence of god. The other passively exists "without" a belief in god. The former is rare because it requires a dogmatic leap of faith not unlike the religionist. The active atheist is no more able to prove the nonexistence of god than the theist is able to prove its existence. The arguments of the agnostic are often the same as the atheist when it comes to disproving the theist's definition of god. The passive atheist is also uncommon and exists simply for lack of introduction to a belief system. The theist, on the contrary, asserts positively the existence of one or more gods.

The "atheist" agnostic is a rationalist "without" a belief in god. He or she does not positively deny such existence but perceives the proposition, "belief in god," as inexplicable. Every attempt to define god develops into contradictions and mutual exclusions. "Theistic" agnostics rationalize that there is a god or gods but the notion is neither defined nor requires definition. Some agnostics, going further than Huxley, rationalize that man "cannot know" if there is a god. It hails from the Kantian arguments postulating the limits of pure reason and sense perception. However, bolstered by the observation of humankind's historical intellectual development, the "cannot know" doctrine limits potential. Our present rational and sentient limitations do not exclude the possibility of future enlightenment. The important thing about agnosticism is that it is more a method of rationalization than a belief or non-belief in god. If one can prove the existence of god, then the term "agnosticism" will become moot and obsolete. Agnosticism requires evidence and proof for a proposition but maintains a humble recognition of personal uncertainty as to the definition and existence of god.

ARISTOTLE'S LOGIC

It takes few words to tell the truth
Chief Joseph Nez Pierce Tribe

There may be heaven and there may be hell;
Meanwhile, we have our life here-Well ?
Anonymous

Before beginning this tent revival for agnostics, I will offer a little instruction on traditional logic formulated by Aristotle back in the third century BCE. Aristotle believed that the unexamined life was the disease and scourge of society. His brilliant life of reflection and argument defeated the academic mode of mechanical acceptance of contemporary myths.

Aristotle divided logic into two branches pragmatically known as inductive and deductive reasoning. Inductive reasoning is the gathering of many individual instances of related facts in order to establish the probability or improbability of a theory. It is the analysis of related pieces of particular information, *a posteriori*, to get to a near certain or probable universal (from the particular to the general) conclusion. For example, Galileo concluded by repetition, observance and inductive reasoning that it is a law of nature that all bodies fall at the same rate of acceleration. A judge or jury uses induction by examining many pieces of gathered evidence to convict or acquit an accused criminal. I have heard people say that they deduced from "all the evidence" that their conclusion was so and so. This is wrong. Whenever evidence is used to build a case, one has used inductive reasoning. Only after one has inferred from "established facts," has one deduced.

Deduction is the analysis of facts already known about some or every member (the universe) of a group, class or species to certify the truth or error of a statement or proposition made about a member of a class. It is reasoning from the general truth or from known facts, *a priori*, in order to get to the bottom or truth of a particular assertion (from the general to the particular). Aristotle defined principles of valid reasoning and argument that, if used correctly, will always come to true conclusions. The masterpiece of deductive reasoning is Aristotle's syllogism.

A simple syllogism is a three sentence argument (two premises and a conclusion) made of statements in one of four forms: "All A's are B's" (universal affirmative); "No A's are B's" (universal negative); "Some A's are B's" (particular affirmative); or "Some A's are not B's" (particular negative). The letters A and B are called "terms." They are simply nouns that represent the subject and object of each sentence. The sentences are called premises or propositions. Each premise must have one term in common with the other premise and one in common with the conclusion. They are categorical in that they describe an action or relation between the terms as, "is" or "is not," "are" or "are not."   Since the three propositions in a syllogism can each be of four different forms, there can be 64 (four to the third power) valid syllogistic arrangements with universal, particular, affirmative, and negative patterns of premises.[2] Once again, a valid syllogism used with facts will always produce a true conclusion.

Hence, the syllogism:

All men are **mortal.**
Thomas Jefferson was **a man.**
Therefore, **Thomas Jefferson** was **mortal.**

A valid syllogism will always be true no matter what terms are used, as long as the premise is a fact and the form is maintained.

Now, then, if a person comes to me and says, Hey . . . It's a fact . . . Thomas Jefferson was mortal. I have the tools to verify this assertion. I can use inductive reasoning by going out and observing the finite nature of mankind and by visiting Thomas Jefferson's grave in order to convince myself that it is beyond doubt that the statement is true. Or I can deduce from facts already known about the history of mankind in order to verify the assertion.

By the same token, if a man comes to me and says that Jesus walked on water, I can use induction and tell you that I have never seen a man walk on water nor have I known anyone who has seen this occur. As a consequence I'm not convinced. In addition, I deduce from the general knowledge already gathered about the density of a man compared to the density of water and can safely say that . . .

No **man** can **walk on water**.
Jesus was said to be a **man**.
It follows then, that **Jesus** did not **walk on water**.

COSMOLOGY

Two things fill the mind with ever increasing wonder and awe, the starry heavens above me and the moral law within me.
Immanuel Kant

What follows from the biblical creation story is an illogical conclusion held by doctrinal fundamentalists and creationists that god frequently snaps his fingers and intervenes like magic to govern our every step in order to fulfill his will. Despite the fact that natural events like the origins of life, thunderstorms, earthquakes, plagues and eclipses all have physical and biological causes and effects, creationists will tell you that it is god's active will and intervention that creates the circumstance. If they pray for relief, let's say rain, and it does rain, they explain it as an act of god in response to their prayer. If it does not rain, they say that god has another reason for not doing it despite their need.[3] Either way, the god-cause explains nothing.

The god cause is accepted by most creationists by assumption and blind faith

...because the *Bible* says so. Surprisingly, there are a handful of creationists who can academically argue their point. They are the few who have found the cosmological argument from Thomas Aquinas. The argument is based on the analysis of cause and effect/prime mover first postulated by Heraclitus of Ephesus (500 BCE) and Aristotle (300 BCE). The Muslim, Averroes, and the Jewish philosopher, Maimonides, applied the same argument to their doctrines during the 13th century.

For its time, Thomas Aquinas' *Summa Theologica,* was absolutely brilliant and delivered the best explanation, based on Aristotle's logic and Church   doctrine, that anyone had   yet to suggest for the nature of god and the universe. It seemed obvious that Aquinas had hit the nail on the head.   But that which at first looked good was debated a few centuries later by other philosophers like Hume and Kant and the cosmological argument was reduced to a leap of faith.

It asserts that . . .

All things that exist have a **cause**.
The **universe** is a **thing that exists**.
Undeniably, the **universe** has a **cause**
(Aquinas' **First Cause**) . . . [4]

And . . . nothing moves without being moved by something else.

This is a valid syllogism except for Aquinas' qualification that I have placed in parentheses. Thomists identify the "cause" of the aforementioned conclusion as the "first cause" and prime mover of the universe, the uncausable cause; *i.e.*, "god." Unnoticeably, Aquinas destroys the validity of the syllogism by the leaping notion that a "cause" could ever be considered a "first cause." Including the term "first cause" changes the syllogism to a sophism. The syllogism is mine. Aquinas did not actually use the syllogism to come up with his conclusion. That would have been impossible since the term "first cause," meaning "god," is not a universal term to which subsets or members belonging to the set can be

derived or deduced. He abused a philosophical tool which, unbeknown to him,
would later be recognized as Ockham's
razor to come up with his desultory conclusion. Thomists skip necessary propositions that should lead to the conclusion of a
"first cause" event horizon (necessary
being) transcending physical experience.
These absent propositions in his reasoning
are the missing links of the cosmology theory.

Immanuel Kant scrutinized the cosmological theory in his *Critique of Pure
Reason* (I provide it as a reference, but only
with the warning that it is a tortuous,
masochistic read). Kant explains that the
methods of empiricism, scientific method,
and induction, from which we derive the
principle of causality, can only be used in
the analysis of the physical world. Cause
and effect derived from observable sense
experience, which relate only to physics,
do not apply to the immaterial objects of
transcendental intellectual ideas.[5] Aquinas
took the principle of causality out of context
by using the observable law of physics, the

natural law of cause and effect, to come up with an unobservable, metaphysical, super- natural "law." The aforementioned syllo- gism belongs to the natural world, and Aquinas' shortcut conclusion to a "first cause" does not.

Again, I grant the premises that each cause is the effect of some precedent and that each effect is the cause of its conse- quent. But I can't draw a rational conclu- sion that there was a supernatural environ- ment before time or that the material world was started by the magic of an uncaused, invisible personality. The causal principle stays in the known physical universe and has no application outside the laws of physics. If one applies the concrete princi- ple of causality, one doesn't arrive scientifi- cally or philosophically at a finite past and then disembark into the fifth dimension of an uncausable cause. Instead, one simply confronts the Conservation Laws of Physics; specifically the First Law of Thermodynamics, that energy and matter can neither be created nor destroyed, only change in form. Matter and energy continue the repetition of transformation throughout the physical universe along the time intervals of an infinite past and future. It is like the decimal equivalent of one-third; it goes on forever as .333. . . .

There is a "big bang" theory which theorizes an event horizon, the border of time in the finite past. Nevertheless, it is identical to the cosmological theory if it postulates something from nothing. The Hubble telescope has identified the existence of billions of galaxies all separated by light years and parsecs from each other. One can verify this through observation and surmise by the laws of physics that each galaxy may have begun by a type of big bang. But a big bang theory without the mention of a pre-existing subatomic environment from which a blast could be induced is merely the magical thinking of the Thomistic first cause/prime mover theory in disguise. Very big bangs of abstract colossal magnitude occur often in our vast universe. Consequently they ignite from pre-existing physical conditions. There would be no "laws" of physics if it were determined that something could come from nothing. We know by these laws that something physical has always existed. As I repeat several times throughout this work, physicists have made a determination that energy and matter cannot be created or destroyed and that only their forms are subject to change. Hence, matter is eternal. From this we can infer that our universe came to us by transformation and not creation. What is there that necessitates the jump to a universe predated by a supernatural world? Can we keep our religious aspirations and expectations in the physical universe? Could a god be natural, as some pantheists believe? I don't know; I am an agnostic.

ATTRIBUTES OF GOD

*For what is faith unless it is to believe what
you do not see?*
St. Augustine

God either does or does not exist. The definition of god is prerequisite to assertion. If you do not know what a "god" is, you don't know what you're looking for much less possess the wherewithal to say that one exists. It is a true dichotomy that you can't say god exists unless you can define it, and you can't define it unless it exists for observation. Through no fault of our own, the effort to define "god" is so far impossible on the level of observation and inference. My agnostic answer to the question of god's existence is . . . "I don't know." And frankly, I am somewhat miffed at the majority that won't join with me and other agnostics in the humble admission of our own ignorance when it comes to defining god.

The truth is, the attempt to define god is self defeating. If one insists on characterizing god as supernatural and unlimited,

one can't define it without causing its fatali-
ty. Once a theist has labeled god with an
attribute, he has given "definition," parameters or borders to that which he defines.
Again, that is okay when defining a natural
god. But if one maintains that god is unlimited, he is stuck with the oxymoron of the
"infinite attribute."   Once you define the
unlimited, you have limited it.[6]

Relinquishing the attempt to define
god in positive terms, some theologians
have attempted to define god in the negative; by what god is "not." As a consequence, when a thing is defined as infinite,
which is another term for not finite; eternal,
i.e., not bound by time; immaterial, i.e., not
material; invisible, i.e., not visible; ineffa-
ble, i.e., not describable; or immutable, i.e.,
not changeable, the ultimate inference is
that it is "not" or nonexistent.[7]

In order to confirm beyond peradven-
ture that the established definitions of god
are implausible, one needs to examine the
positive assertions as to its existence. I will
presently bring forth western religion's self-

contradictory definition of god as the super-natural, omnipotent, omniscient and omni-benevolent creator of all things. The con-clusion, one will see, is that the "god" of this description, *i.e.*, the biblical description, cat-egorically does not exist.

The word "supernatural" is itself merely a concept, an abstract thought, a notion that has no proof of its own reality or existence. Nothing exists that is not natu-ral. If a thing exists that has not yet been observed, it will also come into the set of "all things natural" as soon as it is discov-ered. Things "outside of nature" are only in the mind. The term "supernatural" is a part of the lexicon of faith practitioners, who have guessed, without a shred of evidence and out of the ancestral fear of the unknown, that there exists another dimen-sion outside of the natural universe of per-ceivable laws, causes and effects.

Even if we believed on faith, which the cosmological argument requires by its "something from nothing" suggestion, in the existence of a god creator, the failure of the definition of god given by organized religion is obvious on many arguable fronts. Due to the short supply of talking burning bushes, the cosmological argument lends little corroboration to the allegation that such a god has revealed itself as a personality to individuals and enlightened them as to its own specific attributes. Nothing can be done to overcome the philosophical contradictions that the western definitions of god present.

OMNIPOTENCE

God is a scientist, not a magician.
Albert Einstein

Reflecting on the definition of "omnipotence," we see that it is the single word definition synonymous to most faith practitioners' abstract notion of what "god" is. It means all-powerful. By short-sighted human standards and limited reflection, it most often conveys the simple idea of an instantaneous ability to do anything that is conceivably possible. The opposite is true. Absolute omnipotence is absolute autonomy and completely self satisfied. It needs nothing and is mutually exclusive to the notion of adding anything to its existence. The notion of absolute omnipotence is mutually exclusive to terms such as "need," "want" or "desire" and adjectives such as "offended" or "jealous," which imply needs indicative of impotence, not omnipotence, and weakness, not power. That is to say, the two terms omnipotence and creation are mutually exclusive. Omnipotence can never be unsatisfied. The notion of absolute omnipotence is anti-intuitive because it doesn't allow desire; and creation is the fulfilment of desire.

If we downsize absolute omnipotence to the semi-omnipotent notion of a lonely creator with needs, it still doesn't fit into the universe. For the sake of continuing the argument, we will ignore the notion of a god with emotional needs and concentrate on the omni-ability to bring about the universe without effort, tools, contrivance or time interval.[8] What does that give us? The stumbling block continues in that, even with semi-omnipotence, <u>will</u> and <u>action</u> continue to remain identical. The notion doesn't allow for time interval. The time interval between cause and effect cannot coexist with the notion of omnipotence. And, if omnipotence is the natural law, then the laws of physics are a figment of our imagination and we should all get our heads examined. My point is that creation, at the metaphorical "hands" of a semi-omnipotent god, would <u>not</u> have come into existence by time interval, cause and effect, steps and levels, the observable laws of physics, by the gradual degrees of 14 billion years, a biblical 6000 years or even a six-day work week, because will and action are identical. Therefore, one must exclude omnipotence as the method and source for the expansion of the universe.

Under the influence of our physical reality we can neither escape time interval, which is intrinsic to material change, nor contrivance, which is intrinsic to cause and effect. If we continue to forge a supernatural god, then we are forced to equate omnipotence with magic; the ability to instantly reshape the world in order to fulfill a good servant's prayer. We supply god with the visual notion of finger snapping magic in order to fulfill our dreams and make sense of what we don't understand. The biblical story satisfies this need. It is anthropomorphic in that it depicts the act of creation performed in a manner that man would have done it if he were god (with the inclusion of the creative limitation of needing rest on the seventh day). *Genesis* is written like a Cinderella fantasy with the bigger than life moral lessons of punishment and retribution for uncivilized behavior.

Steering back to the incompatibility of the notion of omnipotence and the reality of time interval and contrivance, I will continue by saying that today is the first day of the rest of the life of the evolving universe. It didn't begin or end as in *Genesis*. The known universe is developing and expanding. The physical and biological world evolves through a series of conditions and alliances in order to function the way it does. Things don't just happen, as would be the case with creation via *semi-omnipotence*. White blood cells and antibodies cure disease, not the finger snapping of an intervening god. The joinder of hydrogen and oxygen by means of positively and negatively charged particles is required for the existence of water. It is not here by the act of an omnipotent god; a god that cannot use the medium of time interval and contrivance. If a creator-god requires a means-to-an-end, then he is not omnipotent. If one accepts the notion of omnipotence one can't accept the laws of nature and vice-versa.

George Smith noted that it is important to realize that within the only existence known to man, *i.e.*, the observable universe, every entity has a specific nature and attribute which limits it to the predictable thing that it is.[9] What we observe is that the universe is bound by known, empirical, and provable laws of physics and biology. It is not unbound by the intervention and coexistence of supernatural omnipotence. Omnipotence conjures a universe of an unintelligible, unpredictable, Disneyesque wonderland where monkeys might fly out of your you-know-what! The intervention of an omnipotent being into the known and physical world would make a sham out of causality and all the laws of physics. Magic and miracles would take the place of order, and science would have no value. The term "rational explanation" would become a meaningless phrase. To accept omnipotence, we must accept effects without natural causes. This means magic.[10] Magic has neither been demonstrated to exist nor ever been observed by science.

Magic is **nonexistent**.
Omnipotence is **magic**.
In that case, **omnipotence** is **nonexistent**

The word "creation" is an abstract notion which has, by suggestion, taken its place as our description of reality. The correct word describing the existence of the universe should be "transformation." I can't think of anything that is actually created, whether it be a star, a planet, a pair of britches or a song (the notes were already there). One cannot validly project the need to create unto a self-satisfied omnipotent god. The notion of creation is spawned by the action of men and beasts who have needs for survival. In this sense, humans create (make) clothes, shelter and government for protection, agriculture for sustenance, companionship for propagation and religion to assuage the psychological need for magic in unanswered questions. To proffer that god would have had a desire to create, or possessed a need at any moment to be adored . . . or could be offended by a sin, would necessarily mean that he would be lacking, needy, vulnerable, imperfect and <u>not</u> omnipotent at some time. These weaknesses fall into the anthropomorphic bailiwick of man's desires and are projected unto an abstract notion of deity and reflected back on man as doctrine in order to control and subordinate other men.

Most religious thinkers claiming the existence of an omnipotent god also claim that the universe has a design. From 18th century Deist apologetics came William Paley's, *Evidences of Christianity.* Today it has morphed into the nomenclature of "intelligent design" and is being promoted to support the *Genesis* story of creation as opposed to the theory of evolutionary transformation. Paley's proof of god's existence by way of correlation to the designer of the pocket watch fails to describe an omnipotent god. According to him, there can be no design without a designer. Beside the fact that he begs the question that the universe is itself a design, Paley merely alludes to cause and effect. The difficulty of a cosmological event horizon reappears, wherein one must jump, like Alice through the looking glass, into the superstitious wonderland of an uncaused creator. Design is just another contrivance which misses the mark. The notion of design exists outside of the set of defined omnipotence.

The same folks that theorize a designed universe must concede to the recognition of its flaws as well. It's a pretty cool universe but it ain't perfect. Concurrent with the mutual exclusion of omnipotence and the inefficiency of cause and effect within the same set, you have the imperfections of a violent universe and the Second Law of Thermodynamics, or Law of Entropy, in which everything cools off, atrophies and breaks down. Aside from the good life, which those of us who have the leisure time to read this book are lucky enough to experience, the known universe, as a whole, is a system of breakdown, pain, suffering, injustice and confusion. Could a perfect design entail automatic breakdown? Could it entail the extinction of dinosaurs and a multitude of other prehistoric and his-toric species? Could a perfect and omnipo-tent god intentionally invent mechanical and biological flaw? The logical answer is no. As I have shown, we must exclude the need for causality and the existence of imperfection in anything known to exist if we claim at the same time that an omnipotent god created it. Does god have to be omnipotent in order to exist? *Je ne sais pas.*

A ***perfect and omnipotent being*** (is one) that creates ***perfect things.***
The ***universe*** has ***imperfect things.***
As a consequence, a ***perfect and omnipotent being*** did not create the ***universe.***

The notion that god is omnipotent . . . therefore he can create things in any manner or in any way he *wants* and *desires*, is irrational. The key words are "want" and "desire." Omnipotent gods can't want or desire anything. To "want" or "desire" indicates weakness, needs, and vulnerability. Omnipotence and disability or weakness are mutually exclusive terms and cannot be joined within the same set. To say that an omnipotent god can perform as a weak god if he *wants* to is a tribute to man's own mental inability to grasp what he at first proposes, *i.e.*, the consequences of omnipotence and its mutual exclusions. This is an attempt to define omnipotence under the influence of physics and time interval. Once again, absolute omnipotence is absolute autonomy and completely self satisfied. That is to say, the terms omnipotence and creation are mutually exclusive. If we insist on the abstraction of a creative god, then we must utilize a term other than "omnipotent" to define god. It is irrelevant how the theologian may attempt to rationalize this type of semi-omnipotence. The theories that god used the biblical method of creation "just-to-throw-us-off" or to "make-us-wonder" or to "demonstrate-his-glory" or to "prove-any-point," creates a god that is outside of the set of absolute omnipotence and autonomy. It is the non-scientific answer for the unknown explanations to the realities of pain and pleasure, right and wrong, life and death.

Going forward, we recognize that the actuality of omnipotence merging with a human body, such as a god-man, (Jesus, for one among many) is impossible because it is rationally self exclusary. This is the penultimate fixation of man creating god in man's own image and it is shared in practically all religions. The notion comes straight from the abstraction of man's mind. The idea was fashioned by the Egyptians through the concept of Osiris the sun god approximately 4500 BCE and by the Eastern Hindus in the Vedic stories of Krishna around the same era. It was developed by Persian Zoroastrianism (1000 BCE) and then through the Greek Dionysus/Bacchanalian mystery rites around 500 BCE. It is a myth that is entirely incompatible with reasoned argument. Omnipotence and the disability of human flesh are mutually exclusive terms and cannot be joined. "It's a divine mystery!" claim the theologians. Well, it certainly is. Like all things that exist, a human being has a specific nature and attributes which limit it to the thing that it is. Omnipotence cannot be limited and joined with human appetites, temptations, needs, or, more especially death, and continue to be defined as omnipotent. The alleged creator cannot become the created. Defining and containing omnipotence within the skin of a man is as self conflicting as defining omnipotence with words. You can't limit omnipotence. If that could be the case, then we could start answering other self defeating philosophical queries such as . . . can god make a rock so heavy that he, himself, can't pick it up?

An ***omnipotent being*** does not have ***limitations.***
A ***human being*** has ***limitations***.
It follows then, that an ***omnipotent being*** is not (cannot be) a ***human being***.

OMNISCIENCE

*Prayer does not change god, but changes
him who prays.*
Soren Kierkegaard

Knowledge, as we know it, involves the experience of acquisition (perceptive effort), time interval and memory. It is acquired and necessitates verification because of the limitation of the senses. No other type of knowledge is known to exist. The abstract notion of omniscience requires the exclusion of effort, acquisition, and time interval. If god had to acquire or verify his knowledge at any time, he could not be omniscient. Accordingly, the notion of knowledge without acquisition is unintelligible and throws one (me) into an agnostic fit. Like the abstract notion of omnipotence, any application of the term omniscience is self defeating.

Western religion takes it on faith that god is all knowing or omniscient. Like Santa, he knows when everybody has been naughty or nice. He knows what you're thinking. The faithful will agree that god knows everything without experience or time interval. They will submit that god's knowledge is not gained through the process of observation despite the fact that, per infallible scripture in *Genesis,* god saw that his creation was good. (Needless to say that the physical world needs physical eyes to behold it.) I will let the literalists and liberals argue over whether scripture is an allegorical description of god's acts. But again, one is engaged here in the method of adorning god with one of man's attributes to the abstraction of a perfect degree. The anthropocentric usage of sight and obser-vation excludes omniscience.

Omniscience is unacquired, absolute knowledge of all things unbounded by time. It has no past, present or future and is mutually exclusive of change, since change denotes time interval. For that matter, to continue the argument we must, again, weaken the absolute to *semi-omniscience* and bind it within the material world par-ameters of the past, present and future. Even with this Wizard-of-Oz-like know-ledge of man's future, the inference and conclusion would mean that the future is as predetermined as the past and neither god nor man can change it. If god knows the future, then it is determined and he can't change it. If he can't change it, by the way, he can't be omnipotent.[11]   In that case, omniscience and omnipotence are mutually exclusive terms.

All things being equal, omniscience and predestination neutralize the notion of freewill. Freewill is the voluntary and spontaneous ability to choose or change one's mind about a future circumstance. We perceive ourselves as having freewill, but an omniscient god can't tolerate it. If god has pre-knowledge, then he has no freewill to change the course of events (answering prayers for instance). He can't have pre-knowledge of his own arbitrary change of mind; otherwise, the change couldn't be arbitrary or executed by use of freewill. If god has freewill, he can't have preknowledge and vice-versa. Thus, freewill and omniscience are mutually exclusive terms. And as a matter of due course, it bears repeating: if god can't freely and arbitrarily change the future (change his mind); he can't be omnipotent.[12]

John Calvin understood the dichotomy of omniscience and freewill when he dogmatized predestination in his *Institutes of the Christian Religion* in 1561.[13] He surmised that omniscience eliminates the notion of freewill and that men are predestined for either heaven or hell. Calvin was correct in his reasoning (within the box of his faith) but cruel in his conclusion. It is an unfortunate fact for the preachers of Jesus' love that god's creatures are divided, through no fault of their own, into two groups: one damned to eternal fire and the other saved for eternal bliss. Paul went before Calvin and corroborated this reasoning when he spoke of those who are "predestined to conform to the image of his son" (Romans 8:29).[14] This ruins the mission of preaching a religion of salvation, hope and love when the unhappy majority have no choice but to burn in hell.

Omniscience excludes the utility of prayer. Prayer is an attempt to change the immutable, omniscient god's mind to act otherwise from a course that his perfect and all-knowing self has already decreed. A perfect, all-knowing god can't change his initial perfect act for better or worse; not only because it was already a perfect act, but because of the previously argued fact that the knowledge, from all eternity, of the outcome of an event results in the elimination of any volition, decision or ability to change the event. The act of granting a wish or a prayer is known in the world of three dimensions as a management decision . . . as my mother would say, "Don't even ask!"

Prayer brings to mind another thing. Everybody up in heaven: god, angels, saints (Santa) and whoever (and in hell, for that matter: Satan, devils, damned souls) are all bestowed with automatic omniscience and omnipotence when they arrive in heaven or hell. Catholicism gives these dudes the ability to hear, see, know and act upon every prayer, thought, word and action of the human race. Saint Jude and all the saints possess the omniscience to see every novena candle burned in their honor and know the wishes of every child who donates a dollar to the candle fund. They have the omnipotence to intervene with a miracle in order to reward the faith of the pleading supplicant.   And Satan, with his evil devil companions, knows your every thought and inclination in order to subtly tempt you to sin. If warranted, he will burst through the laws of nature and deservingly snatch your ass away by some horrible means and drag you to hell. . . . At this point, I think it's only fair to say that it is hard enough to take the time and effort to argue against a single god having infinite attributes, much less trying to figure out why the rest of these demigods have them too. Amen.

The good thing for everybody con-cerned, is that there is at least one benign aspect to the hostility of the notion of omni-science in the universe of time and space. The elimination of the thinking process inherent to omniscience excludes the anthropological notion of judgement when all nonbelievers are going to be examined and damned to hell. The process of judging is purely pragmatic for the function of a civil society in the material world.   Judging is what humans do. Aside from the fact that omniscience infers predestination and elim- inates freewill (culpability for doing anything wrong), **judgement** involves   the time interval of observation, comparison and evaluation.   Remember, the notion of fact gathering and the thinking process are mutually   exclusive   of   omniscience. *Ensuite*, an omniscient god would be incap- able of performing the function of "the last judgement."

Permit me to segue into the argu- ment, like I did with the notion of omnipo- tence, that omniscience embodied in human flesh is a contradiction in terms. Acquired knowledge and omniscience are mutually exclusive terms and can't coexist in the same being. According to the *Gospel of St. Luke*, Jesus "grew" in wisdom and stature during his childhood.   Justly we infer, that he learned or grew in knowledge as he advanced in age and experience. Again, that's what humans do, not omniscient gods. Granted, the human body is a fact gathering machine. The very function of the five senses is to acquire information and turn it into knowledge by means of re-examination and verification. However, the Christian doctrine that Jesus is one part of a triune god possessing unacquired, eternal omniscience is incompatible with the sentient acquisition of knowledge by verification.

An ***omniscient being*** (is one that) has ***unacquired knowledge***.
Human beings do not have ***unacquired knowledge***.
Therefore, an ***omniscient being*** cannot be a ***human being***.

According to the "infallible" *Bible* Jesus had acquired wisdom. Omniscient gods don't have acquired wisdom. Do I need a syllogism?

OMNI-BENEVOLENCE

Love your enemies.
Jesus

If anyone will not welcome you or listen to your words, shake the dust off your feet when you leave that home or town. I tell you the truth, it will be more bearable for Sodom and Gomorrah on the day of judgement than for that town.
Jesus

He that believes in me shall be saved,
He that believes not in me shall be damned.
Jesus

The Judeo-Christian god is supposed to be all good. Yet he supposedly floods the earth and drowns all living creatures, young and old, guilty or innocent, save a few. He rained fire from heaven on whole cities for committing, it is assumed, some sexual perversion, yet afterwards blessed the hero, Lot, with an incestuous romp with his two daughters. Go figure. He sent plagues and pestilence to the entire nation of Egypt and killed innocent first born children. I don't know if one should blame a god or credit the Old Testament writers for creating a myth, but the story goes that Moses, under the inspiration from god, got annoyed with his army for taking captives and commanded his officers: *"Now, Therefore, kill every male, among the little ones, and kill every woman who has known man by lying with him. But all the young girls who have not known man by lying with him, keep alive for yourselves"* (Numbers *31:17-18).*[15] Joshua's army came upon unsuspecting and innocent inhabitants on its way to the promised land and, *"utterly destroyed all in the city, both men and women, young and old, oxen, sheep, and asses, with the edge of the sword" (Joshua 6:21).*[16] World history gives few examples of tyrants which equal such malevolence toward other human beings. Throughout the scriptures petty crimes are punished by bloody revenge. Children are torn apart by bears for making fun of old men. Innocent folk are tortured for the sins of their fathers. Jehovah gets upset over little things and is reported to have killed 70,000 men, women and children because David took a census of Israel (2 Samuel 24).[17]   The entire Old Testament is a continual account of theocratic mass murder.

There is scarce space to recall here the cruelty of the inquisitions, holocausts and ethnic cleansings brought on in the name of god since the New Testament by bible-based religions.There are enough stonings, burnings, tortures and executions to fill an ocean with victims.

People generally know the difference between good and bad.   Otherwise, we could not even set a standard for the qualification that god is good. Reasoning men and women have had a hard time reconciling god's goodness with the biblical portrayal of a murderous god. Add to that the natural disasters that cause so much injustice, destruction, pain and suffering.

Good is that which *benefits mankind*.
The *murder* of innocent children does not *benefit mankind*.
Consequently, *murder* is not *good*.

According to the *Bible*, **god** commands the **murder of children**.
The **murder of children** is not **good**.
If god commands the **murder of children**, god is not **good**.

The gospel story of Jesus' forgiveness, peace and love is a contradiction in terms to his wrath and eternal torture promised for nonbelievers. The indoctrination by coercion is very plainly spoken in his verbal threat that, *"He that believeth and is baptized shall be saved; but he that believeth not shall be damned" (Mark 16:16).* And, *"He who is not with me is against me" (Luke 11:23).*

George Smith came up with an excellent line of reasoning when he stated: *"If god does not know that there is evil, he is not omniscient. If god knows there is evil but cannot prevent it, he is not omnipotent. If god knows there is evil and can prevent it but desires not to, he is not omni-benevolent. If, as Christians claim, god is all-knowing and all-powerful, we must conclude that god is not all good. The existence of evil in the universe* (which even includes the alleged acts of god himself) *excludes this possibility.*"[18] (Emphasis in parentheses added.)

SACRED WRITINGS

The act of inspired composition, whether of a Blake or a Whitman or a biblical patriarch, whether of the West or the East, appears to be a universal human endeavor, not restricted to one people or religion.
Willis Barnstone

No plausible argument for god's existence can come from the so-called truths in any religious organization's sacred writings. One can argue the interpretation of a belief relative to a religion's particular doctrine printed in its scriptures, but one cannot take for granted the truth of its revelation. We don't put the cart before the horse by assuming something is true, like "the existence of god," from something that is written by men.

It is not a valid argument to say that god exists because the *Hindu Vedic Books,* The *Avesta*, the *Koran of Mohamed*, the Jewish *Torah*, the *Talmud* or the *Bible* says so. Such a strategy fails because it begs the questions at issue: Does a supreme being exist and are the contents themselves revealed by such a being? To open an argument with:

The contents of a book are revealed by god.
Therefore, god exists.

. . . is fatuous. One must prove that god exists first and then argue the merits of proof of a revelation.

The *Bible* has been heralded as infallible by Catholicism, more especially by Pope Leo XIII in his 1893 encyclical, "*Providentissimus Deus*," and by the American Baptists of the tent revival era of the 1870's. However, to call the *Bible* infallible is an unjustified act. By what standard and by what authority has this book been deemed infallible? From *Genesis* to *Revelation* or the *Apocalypse*, its doctrines and accounts of events uphold a standard of contradictions. In addition, the majority of its *Old and New Testament* books have no known authors. Yet it has been the basis of authority for the existence of god, the institution of governments, and the perpetration of the cruelest wars, inquisitions and perfidious acts on humanity.

I discuss the issue of biblical infallibility because I am an agnostic and the inconsistencies in the *Old and New Testaments* are part of the reason why I am so. Judaism, Islam and Christianity are *Old and New Testament Bible*-based religions. My argument will apply specifically to them.

THE OLD TESTAMENT

Oh Bible, say I, what follies and monstrous barbarities are defended in thy name.
Walt Whitman

The *Bible* story is the Judeo/Christian account of god's law and his historical inter-action with the universe and the human race. It was good for the superstitions of its day, when it was penned incrementally by a bevy of known and unknown authors between the tenth century BCE and the third century CE. It afforded a divine expla-nation of events that fit the bill until science came along.

The *Bible* relates that god decided to create the universe one Sunday morning, about 4004 years (an estimate produced from scriptural genealogies) before Jesus' alleged birth. Carbon 14 dating techniques have calculated the ages of certain dead things up to 60 thousand years. However, its use has often been controversial because of the misuse of environmental contingencies. Meanwhile, modern scien-tists have utilized more accurate radiometric calculations of the half life of uncontaminated isotopes to give a range of 4.2 to 4.5 billion years for the existence of our solar system. Also, astronomers have deduced the age of some visible stars outside of our solar system to be approximately 14 billion years old by using the known ratio of velocity to distance in the expansion of the universe (the Hubble Constant). There are also less complicated geological tangibles that produce the age of sediments and precious stones far in excess of the biblical math. I have visited the Luray caverns in the mountains of Virginia and personally seen the 47 feet tall columns of stalagmites and stalactites that geologists calculate to be seven million years old using the plausible rate of formation at one square inch of sediment per 120 years. Yet the creation credo prevails over modern science in the heart and mind of the confident biblicist who insists on a six thousand year old universe.

Some *Bible* scholars acknowledge the time interval of science and theorize that the truths of the sacred books are captured in allegory. They say we don't know what a day means to god. A thousand years could be a day to god's meaning of the term. Well . . . I'm too impatient to argue that point in detail because it is just dense. If a supernatural god hosts the universe, time interval by any standard is moot. Schedules come from man and are projected unto the abstract notion of god. Nevertheless, I want to toy briefly with the word "allegory" as an interesting notion.

The term "allegory" should be an agonizing topic for literalists since it is the utilization of symbolics to represent abstract ideas. Allegory is a figure of speech which refers to only a similarity of the literal; something that it does not literally describe. Allegory is not the truth. It is an approximation. It is intrinsic to the religious works of all faiths for the simple reason that symbols, parables and metaphors are the only literary tools that can be used to explain the abstract, that which can only exist in man's mind. The existence of allegory feeds agnosticism and supports the argument against biblical infallibility.

Allegory cannot be infallible since it is not literal. Allegory is a figment of one's imagination; in this case, a simulacrum of the indefinable. Infallibility denotes literal truth. The *Bible* may be infallibly allegorical but not allegorically infallible. It may also be literally allegorical but not allegorically literal. It is not literally infallible because it is not infallibly literal. Got it? Good! (It's fun being an agnostic.) The allegorical methodology of religious works only confuses the issue of substance and minimizes the literalist's claim that his or her particular sacred book is an infallibly inspired text.

Going back to the topic of *Genesis,* the book reveals exactly what god accomplished on each day of creation before he finished and rested. There are two distinct *Bible* versions of the order of creation. Scholars refer to them as *Genesis* one and two. They suspect that they were authored by two different scribes at two different times. Take note that the chronological order of *Genesis* "one" creates heaven and earth, light, separation of earthly and heavenly waters, seas and dry land, plants, sun and stars, fish and birds, land animals, and humans last. It is interesting to note that, except for the mixup of putting the creation of the sun and stars on the fourth day after the creation of light, the chronology of the six days of creation appears to follow Darwin's chronology of biological evolution with the progression of vegetation, fish, land animals, and finally man. I grant that in this instance, a vague correlation exists between the biblical explanation and sci-ence. The creation order of *Genesis* "two" is sequenced as: heaven and earth, man, then trees and the Garden of Eden, animals and birds, and finally woman. This order is not just supplemental, but chronologically different from *Genesis* "one" and thus excludes infallibility.

Apply the story of Noah's Ark to com-mon sense and natural science. Yes, much of the earth has been immersed and sculpt-ed by water. Most of the earth today is cov-ered by water. However, there has never been any scientific evidence that the entire earth was completely covered by water within the last six thousand years or at any one time. How does one possibly reason that Noah, at the age of six hundred years, took off on a boat with his family and every species of living creature that exists today and lived on it for nearly twelve months until stepping out on dry land? That's a lot of bullshit. (Couldn't pass that up!) The largest human carrying ship that exists today is a US military aircraft carrier. It holds about six thousand personnel and can feed them for approximately ninety days. Even that is not big enough to hold and feed the two million pairs of known species of land mammals, birds, reptiles, and marsupials in existence today. Accordingly, every land animal on the earth outside the ark perished. Only the passengers on the ark survived. Just the opposite, there are microbes, insects and creatures today, and races of human beings for that matter, that are climate, continent and habitat specific. They had scarce time or ability to hoof it over to the Mideast to catch Noah's ark and afterwards make their way back to their present places of environmental enclosure.

After the flood, sometime within the alleged four thousand year period between Christ and creation, the eight rescued members of Noah's family scattered from the ark abandoned on Mt. Ararat to their "native" lands and morphed into Australian aborigines, Inuit Eskimos, African Negroes, Asian Japanese, and European Caucasians, etc. The literalists hate evolution, but if they are going to believe in that story, then Mel Gibson will have to make another movie called, *"The Greatest Evolution Story Ever Told."*

Just as unbelievable, the Galapagos tortoises, which I don't think even swim, made it back to their islands. The kangaroos and koalas made it over to Australia. The lemurs swam to Madagascar and the tapers traveled back over the Bering Strait to Argentina. Even the sloth, the slowest mammal on the planet, made it back to the Amazon jungle before humans did. It's a shame that I must verbalize it, but the story of Noah's ark is simply not credible to the person who has a modicum of education and trusts his or her own senses.

The storyteller's account of our solitary progenitors, Adam and Eve, and then again Noah's family, did not anticipate the refutation of this claim by the future discovery of DNA which provides proof that only six tenths of 1 percent of our genome differs from that of the chimpanzee. DNA may some day lead to an irrefutable proof of the evolutionary origins of all species.

Messy physics and biology aside, the same basic interpretations in the *Bible* of the origins of the universe were held by the Gnostic Egyptians, Sumerians and Persians before the Hebrew scribes of the Babylonian captivity put pen to paper or "ink to papyri" and gave their account. *Genesis* and the Persian *Zend-Avesta* relate identical chronologies in their creation stories, only the time interval is different.[19] It would be logical to suspect that the Hebrew authors drew much of their religious experience and belief from their captors during the Babylonian captivity. But the origins of an infallible text couldn't come from a pagan culture now, could it?

It is interesting to note that, despite the doctrine of monotheism that the Jews and Christians profess, the *Bible* contradicts this standard by prescribing a polytheistic belief not unlike the Persians, their fellow co-habitants of the time and region. The *Bible* quotes god as saying, "man has become like one of us, knowing good and evil" (Gen 3:22). The *Genesis* usage of the plural form "Elohim," meaning "gods" and other allusions to vestiges of imbibed polytheism were part of the reason that common folk, who would read it at face value, were not permitted by the monotheistic Catholic Church to read Scripture themselves.   Lay people were not allowed access to scripture until after Martin Luther and the protestant revolution.   Today, of course, face value has been theologized through Christian apologetics into the unintelligible doctrine of the Trinity, one god in three persons.

The five books of the *Pentateuch: Genesis, Exodus, Leviticus, Numbers, and Deuteronomy*, or the five books of Moses, were not written by Moses. They have no known author. The once widely accepted belief that Moses authored these books has diminished since the writings of researchers and philosophers like Thomas Paine and Bertrand Russell eliminated any doubt. In all probability, the authorship of the first five books of the *Old Testament* dates to unknown Hebrew scribes sometime after the reign of all of the Jewish kings, during the time of the Babylonian captivity. If one examines the genealogy of the descendants of Esau, called the Edomites, recited in the first book of the *Old Testament, Genesis* 36:31-40, "*and these are the kings that reigned in Edom, before there reigned any king over the children of Israel . . .*" and then reads the first chapter of *First Chronicles*, beginning at the 43rd verse, allegedly written about one thousand years later, one can see without doubt that these ten verses are **word for word** the same in each book. This genealogy of kings found in *Genesis* is copied and pasted from *Chronicles*. Thus, *Genesis* and *Chronicles* were written by the same author or co-authored after the reign of Zedeckiah, who was carried captive to Babylon by King Nebuchadnezzar about 588 BCE, almost one thousand years after Moses' death.[20] Writing the stories of *Genesis* with the life and times of Moses 1000 years after their occurrence would be like having a contemporary author attempt to write the life and times of Charlemagne with few references, and those only by word of mouth. It would scarce be infallible and its precision would rest on the names of very distant and unreliable sources.

Moreover, the uncertainty as to the authors of scripture is evidenced by the cutting and pasting of verses within the books of *Ezra* and *Chronicles*. The first three verses of *Ezra* and the last two of *Chronicles* are the same. See for yourself.[21]

Few, if any, of the prophetic books, psalms or proverbs of the *Bible* were written entirely by the same authors. The books of *Joshua* and *Samuel* both describe happenings after their deaths. Hence we infer, they were not the authors of these books. The *Book of Isaiah* reflects almost 200 years of Israelite history from 700 BCE to after the Babylonian exile of 539 BCE. It is necessarily true then, that Isaiah could not have been the sole author of the book ascribed to him. It is an error to call David the author of the *Psalms* when the *137th Psalm* describes distinctly the sorrow of the Babylonian captivity, which took place more than 400 years after David.[22]

If you take away authorship from the books of the *Bible,* the alleged conduit of god's revelation in the first person, they become anonymous and spurious. I submit: The word authority comes from the word author.

> ***Authority*** (is a thing that) ***has authorship***.
> Most of the Bible ***books*** do not ***have authorship***.
> Thus we infer, those ***books*** have no ***authority***.

They have no authority and there can be little weight given to their credibility. The stories of Adam and Eve, Noah's Ark, the Tower of Babel, the accounts of giants and men living more than 900 years, the life and miracles of Moses, the prophets and later, Jesus, afford no more credibility than the Greek and Roman mythologies, the Hindu Vedic books or the Persian *Avesta*.

THE NEW TESTAMENT

Most people are bothered by those passages in Scripture which they cannot understand; but as for me, I always noticed that the passages in Scripture which troubled me most are those which I do understand.
Mark Twain

The first known public appearance of Christian writings are the *Epistles of Paul,* samples of which scholars say were written around 50 CE. Surprisingly, Paul doesn't recount (except for allusions to the crucifixion and resurrection) a single incident of Jesus' life. Paul's Christ is a timeless mythical figure, not unlike the contemporary pagan Dionysus.[23] Even though he was not an eyewitness, one would think that Paul, if he had been acquainted at all with the gospel Jesus, could not have resisted relating some of Jesus' living examples of divinity and miracles which encompassed almost every interaction he had with humanity.

I submit that the literal biography of Jesus came after the spirituality of an enigmatic Jesus myth.[24] The New Testament books are set up in a manner to give the appearance that the *Gospels*, a biography of Jesus, came before the publication of the spiritual precepts of Christianity, when in fact, the opposite occurred.[25] The evidence of the second century arrivals of *Matthew, Mark, Luke* and *John,* in classical Greek, casts doubt on the claim that the stories were set before the doctrines of the spiritual life were developed. This evidence also calls into doubt the tradition that the *Gospels* were written by eyewitnesses to a life that ended around 30 CE, authors who were allegedly Judean, Aramaic speaking, provincial folk.

After the first works of Paul, more than twenty years pass before Jesus is given an historical and geographical setting by the *Gospel of Mark* between 70 CE and 110 CE.[26] Mark doesn't claim to be a witness to the life of Jesus; in fact, the early church had problems with treating his work as canonical because he was said to be no more than an assistant or translator for Peter.[27] The German scholar, Karl Ludwig

Schmidt, was able to demonstrate in 1919, how the *Gospel of Mark* had been constructed from pre-existing fragments. The Berlin philologist, Karl Lachmann, in conjunction with other biblical scholars, concluded that the *Gospels* of *Matthew* and *Luke,* which appeared between 90 CE and 135 CE, were make-overs of *Mark*, which was the earliest and most basic *Gospel*.[28] Luke, besides, known traditionally as a gentile physician and disciple of Paul, never saw Jesus. Matthew and John are traditionally accepted as eyewitnesses to Jesus. However, the *Gospel of Matthew* is evidently a merged addition to *Mark*. The *Gospel of John* appears long after his death, begging the question of authenticity. In addition, John's *Gospel* exhibits a sophisticated development of Greek philosophy through his borrowed use of the Logos and a stand out separation from Jewish origins; all of which undermine the position that the *Gospel* accredited to him was written by an uneducated Judean fisherman. The *Gospel of John* is believed by certain scholars to be the work of the Gnostic Cerinthus.[29]

Who is to say, then, since: *Mark* was created from already existing fragments by a non-witness to Jesus' life; *Luke* was a remake of *Mark* by a nonwitness; *Matthew* was a remake of *Mark*; and *John* was a probable forgery based on obvious incongruent time and subject matter . . . that any of the four *Gospel* writers knew a historical Jesus first hand? It takes faith to do so.

There is evidence offered in the book *The Jesus Puzzle*, by Earl Doherty, that the gospels were written by a procedure of Jewish story telling called *Midrash*. By this method writers take passages from Old Testament prophecies and create a story around them.[30]   In any event, unknown members of the religious communities of the *Old and New Testaments* were the authors of their own scriptures. Answering to nobody but themselves they developed them, used them and canonized them. The twenty-seven books of the existing *New Testament* were only a fraction of the literary output in the first three centuries of Christianity.   *Gospel* stories carrying the names of the apostles were widely circulated among developing Christian populations during that time. These books maintained the early Christian appetite for miracles and revelations. A low estimate of at least one hundred gospels was in circulation before a codified scripture came forth.

The discovery at Nag Hamadi, Egypt, of the Christian Gnostic manuscripts in 1945 received a lot of notoriety. The thirteen leather bound papyrus Coptic texts were filled with pre-institutional Christian beliefs that no one knew existed.[31] Some of the works included were the *Gospel of St. Thomas*, which contains 114 sayings of Jesus which he allegedly passed on to Thomas; the *Gospel According to Hebrews*, the *Letters of Eugnostos*, the *Infancy Stories of Thomas*, and the *Acts of Pilot*. These gospels were hidden in the local caves in earthen jars because the contents were forbidden material. Gnostic writers consistently portrayed the story of Jesus as an allegorical figure of the spiritual life and not as a literal historical figure. Their spirituality contained no hard and fast doctrine and included pagan concepts in a less than systematic path to union with god. They were the first Christians from which literalism evolved. As the literalists emerged the Gnostics struggled to maintain their right to personal and independent interpretation of religious belief. Their voices disappeared.

Opposition to literal Christianity ended after the ascendency of Constantine as Roman emperor in 306 CE. He became institutionalized as the "Holy" Roman Emperor after he presided over the council of Nicaea in 325 CE. He was holy, yet, history has it that he murdered his own stepmother, Fausta, and son, Crispus, for their involvement in a suspected conspiracy which threatened his throne. In the effort to unify the empire under one religion and state government, Constantine backed the Holy Roman Catholic Church against any opposition to its doctrine.

During a brief interim, Julian (355 CE), Constantine's cousin, became Emperor of Rome and tried to reorganize Greco-Roman paganism after the pattern of the new Christian church's hierarchy.

Posthumously, after his early death during a battle in Persia, he was immortalized as "Julian the Apostate" by our unchosen historians. If he had lived longer, Christianity may not have come down to us as the religion that it is today. His short-shrifted attempt to reinstate the past was not repeated. Further opposition to institutional Christianity, especially Roman Catholicism, has since been severely suppressed, and the Churches, most notably the Greek Orthodox and the Roman, have been able to write the book of Christian doctrine and history without contest. From Constantine on, with little interruption, Western Europe's government and the Holy Roman Catholic Church have been united in the enforcement of civil and religious law. The doctrine of the divine right of kings developed and both the Church and state reigned in unity throughout Western Europe for well over a thousand years.

At this point I must digress even more from *New Testament* origins and address a common topic. Some people, in order to defend the divine origin of Christianity, will ask and answer the question: "If Christianity isn't from god, how could it have spread so far and lasted so long?". . . and their own answer, without reflection, is that this is a miracle of persistence which goes to prove that its foundation is divine and that its existence is the will of god. Every religious practitioner of every religion asks the same question and answers in like manner.

My own answer to the previous question is different. It is a natural explanation for the phenomena of institutional persistence based on the observation of history. It applies to the longevity of every religion and it infers and cautions: Make no mistake. Might makes right! If you can't beat it, you join it. On a universal basis, up until the last two hundred years of recorded history, religious institutions have been temporal powers with enforcement capabilities. And when the might of culture is legally enforced by "do or die" principles, the masses generally obey and imbibe the self-enforcing myth which that culture promotes. That situation will persist until the historically installed central power weakens. The tribal and national xenophobia fades at the borders first through the dilution of exposure to different ideas. Then, eventually, the core belief erodes.

This tendency to fade at the borders is relevant to the so-called miraculous permanency of Christianity. The suggestion of doctrinal permanency is a fallacy. Christianity has not remained the same. Religious doctrine based on faith cannot remain static. It is always dynamic. It adjusts as it is imported and exported through the frontiers of time, nationalities and languages. Doctrines adjust when portions become reduced to myth by scientific discovery. Doctrines adjust in every religion and split off into divergent sects of differing interpretations and methodologies. The Roman Catholic Church's (infallible) doctrines have changed in the last 45 years with some of its modern acceptance of science and the mixture of interfaith worship. How many Christian sects are there? Muslim sects? Jewish? Buddhists? And so on. Divide and conquer is what religion generally does best, but it does so at the cost of its doctrinal purity and originality.

Going forward on *Bible* evolution one sees a lot of arbitrary developments as to its formation.   Origen (185-254 CE), the most accomplished Christian scholar of his time, lamented the fact that there was so much diversity in biblical manuscripts due to the scribes who added and deleted as they pleased.[32] Out of the examination of more than 3,000 early texts scholars have observed the evolution of the *Gospels*. Whole sections have been added to earlier writings. One example of this was discovered in the *Gospel of Mark.*   It originally ended in the description of the amazement of the women at the discovery of the empty tomb of Jesus.   That ending eventually became Chapter 13:8 after Church scribes added punctuation, chapter and verse. The long version, which is accepted today, continues and ends with verse 20 as it carries over to the description of Jesus' appearances to his disciples after his resurrection. This extension is not in the early manuscripts.[33]

The first notice of the twenty-seven recognized books of the present *New Testament* comes to us from a record of the 39th Lenten Sermon of St. Athanasius, Bishop of Alexandria, in 367 CE after the reign of Constantine. In 382 CE, Pope Damasus commissioned St. Jerome to translate the *Bible* into Latin which was then called *The Vulgate.* Vowels had to be supplied to the words of the ancient Hebrew script of the *Old Testament.* Punctuation and verse were eventually added to both *Testaments* in the fifth and sixth centuries. There are no records to show how the Church adopted its final version of what was and what was not sacred scripture. Many of the incongruities and contradictions found today in the *Old and New Testaments* stem from the early Christian monk scribes who had full license to cut and paste, modify and embellish the religious text in order to respond to contemporary heresy before any historical codification.

The first English translation of the *Bible* came in 1382, by John Wycliff of

England.   Afterwards, William Tyndale of England translated it from Greek to English in 1525.   His style and use of "thou, thou art, thy and thine," was adopted by King James I for his namesake *Bible* which he commissioned to be printed in 1611.   In fact, the "thou and thou art" style was so catchy that the Angel Maroney also adopted it in America in 1827, when he translated the golden plates of the *Book of Mormon* from Egyptian hieroglyphics into English for Joseph Smith. But I'm not going there. The redundency of religious linguistic styles throughout differing religious creeds is a study of the commonality of religions all in itself.

THE INFALLIBLE GOSPELS

The dogma of the infallibility of the Bible is no more self evident than is that of the infallibility of the Popes.
Thomas Henry Huxley

The four *Gospels* relate differences on the details of many events. These minutiae are no big deal in themselves. Stories usually do change a little when retold by different folks. Unfortunately, faith practitioners ruin a good book and their own reputation for credibility by proclaiming the *Bible* a literal infallible work. The *Bible*, itself, does not claim its own infallibility. Nevertheless, the claim to infallibility can only be fleshed out by scrutiny of some of the varying depictions of the same events retold.

To cite some *New Testament* inconsistencies, we begin with the first chapter of *Matthew* and the third chapter of *Luke*. They give the genealogies of Jesus from David through Joseph's line of descendants. Matthew lists 28 generations by name and Luke lists 42 by name. The only names in common between the two

genealogies are Joseph at the beginning
and David at the end.[34] One does not need
a syllogism to conclude that if Matthew was
infallible and inspired by god then Luke was
not, or vice versa. In any event, one can
see from a perusal of the first pages of the
Bible that it would be an error to assume its
infallibility.

Matthew's accounts are always more
miraculous and grandiose than the other
three writers. Taking, for example, the relation of the passion of Christ, the others
failed to observe and write about the earthquake, the rocks renting, the temple veil rip-
ping from top to bottom, the graves opening
and the bodies of the saints waking from
the dead and strolling along the streets of
Jerusalem during the crucifixion of Jesus.
No chronologists contemporary to the time
corroborate the claim of earthquakes, day
time darkness or any of the other fantastic
allegations. In defense, it is easy enough to
say that these additions don't contradict
the other evangelists and are only cumulative.   However, that is not a credible
defense to consistency. The account of the

discovery of the resurrection at Jesus' tomb is different from all sides.

Matthew, again, goes into a whole story that the others don't relate about the Jews arranging a guard and sealing the tomb and then later paying off the guards to say that the disciples took the body while they slept. (If the guards were sleeping how would they know that the disciples took the body? Did Matthew really miss that?) Anyway, my point is about what the four infallible authors say relating the resurrection scene. **Matthew** relates that there was a great earthquake and an angel of the Lord descended, appearing like lightning, clothes white as snow, rolled back the stone and sat upon it. Mary Magdalene and the other Mary and two people came to see the sepulcher and while one angel was sitting <u>outside</u> of the tomb on top of the stone, he told them that Christ had risen. The women hurried off. They met Jesus on their way, and he told them to get everybody over to <u>Galilee</u> where he would meet them. **Mark** cites Mary Magdalene, Mary the mother of James, and Salome, going to the tomb. They enter the tomb and are told by one young man dressed in white, sitting inside to the right, that Jesus has risen and that they should go to Galilee to meet him. **Luke** states that it was Mary Magdalene, Joanna, Mary the mother of James and the others, more than four who went to the tomb.   Here two men inside the tomb in clothes that gleamed like lightning told them Jesus had risen.   That same day Jesus appeared to the eleven in Emmaus near Jerusalem and not in Galilee. **John** recounts that Mary Magdalene makes two trips to the tomb. On the first trip there were no angels, just an empty tomb and she goes and tells Peter and John that she doesn't know where they took Jesus. They go to the tomb and confirm that it is empty. Peter and John, not mentioned by the other gospels   leave while Mary Magdalene sticks around. She looks into the tomb and two angels in white sitting on each side where Jesus had lain greet her. Then she turns around and Jesus is there and greets her. That same evening Jesus meets the disciples behind closed doors at an undis-closed location. (Probably not Galilee since it is seventy miles away from Jerusalem and too far to walk in a day.)[35]   One must perforce see the mutual exclusion, and not just cumulative relation, these separate texts have for each other.

Infallibility is a **uniform, consistent thing**.
The **Bible** is not a **uniform or consistent thing**.
Without doubt then, the **Bible** is not **infallible**.

The authors of the gospels have Jesus himself making false predictions about the end of the world in *Mark 9:1, "Truly I say to you, there are some standing here who will not taste death before they see the kingdom of god come with power."* In the remake of *Matthew 24: 29-34* he makes the same mistake: he states: *"Immediately after the tribulation of those days the sun will be darkened, and the moon will not give off its light, and the stars will fall from heaven . . .   Then will appear . . . The son of man coming on the clouds of heaven with power and great glory . . .*

Truly, I say to you, this generation will not pass away till all these things take place" (emphasis added).[36] Time for another syllogism:

A ***person that predicts things that do not come true*** is not ***a prophet or infallible***.
Jesus allegedly was a ***person that made predictions that did not come true***.
Consequently, ***Jesus*** was ***not a prophet or infallible***.

If the writers of the books of the *New Testament* had gone separately into one of today's courtrooms in order to testify as to an exact account of the life of Jesus and their own writing's infallibility, their testimony would have been impeached and the case would have been dismissed on the contradiction of their separate stories.

MISSING SECULAR HISTORY OF JESUS

The shocking fact is that hardly any-body contemporary to the time-frame of Jesus' alleged existence wrote about him. His crucifixion is not among any Roman records. A few historians made mention of the self-evident existence of Christians in the empire. Not surprisingly only one known author makes slight mention of the actual Christ. Tacitus, in his *Annals*, 112 CE, wrote that, "*Their originator, Christ, had been executed in Tiberius' reign by the procurator of Judea, Pontius Pilate.*"[37]   In contradiction, everyone knows that Pilate was the "prefect" of Judea and not the "procurator." This slight mistake in terms allows us to assume that he got his infor-mation from the hearsay of the times instead of any Roman records.[38]

The following is a list of famous pagan writers and historians within the first century who make no mention of Jesus:

Arrian; Pliny the Elder; Pliny;
Suetonius; Martial; Petronius;
Appian; Plutarch; Seneca;
Juvenal; Apollonius; Dion
Pruseus; Theon of Smyrna;
Pausanius; Valerius Flaccus;
Damis; Ptolemy; Florus Lucius;
Silius Italicus; Dio Chrysostom;
Quintilian; Aulus Gelius;
Hermogeones; Favorinus;
Statius; Lysius; Lucanus;
Columella; Valerius Maximus.[39]

Among Jewish historians, Philo the
philosopher, who lived at the same time as
Jesus, makes no mention of him; although,
he makes frequent mention of Pontius
Pilate in his historical works.[40] Justus of
Tiberius, another historian who lived near
Capernaum at the same time that Jesus is
alleged to have been famous, wrote a con-
temporary history and never mentioned
Jesus.[41]

Josephus, the pro-Roman Jewish his-
torian, has become the foundation for
Christian apologetics on the historicity of
Jesus. In opposition, critical analysis has

raised vehement denial over the authenticity of the paragraph wherein Josephus writes of Jesus as the messiah and makes mention of his miracles and crucifixion in his *"Antiquities of the Jews"* circa 101 CE. The paragraph, which could be eliminated without destroying the flow of his historical theme, appeared sometime in the *Antiquities* within the 100 year period between the writings of the Christian scholar, Origin, who comments on the absence of Jesus in Josephus' works in the 3rd century, and Bishop Eusebius, who suddenly produced the passages, in the 4th century.[42]

Josephus was a pharisee born shortly after Jesus' placement in history. He was a soldier in the Jewish forces in Galilee at the time of the Jewish uprising against Rome in 66 CE. Controversy surrounds his reasons for living in Rome the rest of his life. It is alleged that he collaborated with the Roman army and fled to Rome for fear of retribution from his fellow Jews. He believed in the messianic promise and he wrote in contempt for the many imposters of his time.[43]

Aside from the argument of authenticity wherein arises the inference that somebody, other than Josephus, placed the mention of Jesus, "the messiah," into "*The Antiquities of the Jews*," my personal skepticism of its authenticity comes from the fact that Josephus was not a Christian. If Josephus acknowledged the miraculous existence and role of the messiah in Jesus, why, then, wasn't he a convert to Christianity at the time he wrote the passage?

Reliable history is **supported by objective, unbiased references**.
The biography of a literal Jesus is not **supported by objective, unbiased references.**
Thus we infer, **the biography of a literal Jesus** is not **reliable history**.

MEDITERRANEAN PHILOSOPHIES AND GOD-MEN

There is undeniable evidence of the outside cultural influences that go in to make up the so called, divinely inspired, Christian creed and synoptic tradition. In the first place, no one can deny that its written origins are entirely in classical Greek. This, despite the fact that the lives of Jesus and the apostles allegedly took place in the Aramaic speaking Roman occupied Judea. The sustainable reason for the use of Greek instead of the local patois is that the Christian sect originated as a messianic Jewish sect influenced (Hellenized) by the academically Greek diaspora. Many dispersed Jews, exemplified in the writings of the philosopher Philo of Alexandria (20 BCE - 50CE), spoke and wrote in classical Greek. Many of these Jews had their own gnostic traditions and reconciled the gnosis of the Greek gods and mystery cults with the gnosis of Yahweh and the Essenes. Paul, of course, is an exemplar of this set of authors.

The author of the *Gospel of John* (120 BCE) is theologically admired for the use of the *Logos* in the opening passages of his work.   Some less instructed Christians may think that the term *Logos* or "word" made flesh, originated by god's revelation to John.   On the contrary, he is one of many religious philosophical authors to have used the term.   The *Logos* was used extensively in the works of the Greek metaphysicians and hermetic religious cults after Heraclitus of Ephesus (500 BCE) coined the term in reference to his definition of god.   Philo of Alexandria, thought to be the greatest Jewish philosopher of his age, borrowed heavily on the use of the *Logos* in relating god's energy and sources of mediation between god and mankind.   Philo was the first to give it a personified essence in descriptions which mirror the conflicts between the Essenic children of the light and the powers of darkness.   According to the author, James Still, the *Logos* was an intricate part of Greek thought.   He theorizes that the *Gospel of John* was a direct effort to attract the classically educated non-Jews and   those who might reject

Christianity because of its affiliation to the strictures of Judaism. By replacing references of Jesus' Judaic origins with practical implementation of the *Logos* to human spirituality, the author made Christianity more attractive to a larger and more diverse cultural pool. The author, Still, calls this treatment the "Hellenization of Jesus."[44]

Moreover, Paul's epistles put into the context of Christianity a spirituality already practiced by the initiates of the pagan religions. The names of Attis, Mithra, or Dionysus could conceivably replace the name of Jesus in Paul's epistles since their spiritual doctrines were much the same. Christianity and the pagan religions involved the blood sacrifice of their alleged sons of god. They require the spiritual death to self of their members and a baptism of water and fire to initiate their members into the new life of spiritual quest. The terminology of the "children of light" and the "powers of darkness" are contained in the religious writings of the Persians, Greeks and Gnostic Jews. Paul's doctrine of predestination, his accounts of being caught up to the third heaven and his references, in Greek, to the "Archons" are Gnostic concepts and not a part of today's Roman Catholic doctrine. The Catholic Church eliminated the Gnostics and their openly publicized writings in the fourth century.

The similarity of the *Gospel* stories to the pagan stories of miraculous god-men spawned debates between the educated second century pagan and Christian faithful. The disagreement between the early apologists, the pagan Celsus and the Christian Tertulian, concluded briefly when the Christian theologian replied that the coincidence of beliefs rested in a satanic plot of "diabolical mimicry," and that god permitted it in order to test the faith of Christians. Such was the only argument proffered to the inquiring minds of that time.[45]

Diabolical mimicry was an entertaining answer, but it didn't prove anything. The implication today, for reasoning people, is that all of the similar pagan myths had been circulating for centuries before the story of Jesus. It is consequently true, that if any "diabolical mimicry" had been committed, it had been done by the writers of the *Gospels* and not vice versa. It is, besides, a historically repeated social phenomenon that the exportation of a religious belief into another culture incurs a mixture of the importing culture's belief system.

Timothy Freke and Peter Gandy in their book, *The Jesus Mysteries*, chronicle a long list of god-men incarnations whose mythic biographies are a mirror of the Christian Gospels. The most closely related mythic god-men, among many, were Mithra of Persia, Osiris of Egypt, and Dionysus of Greek origin. Their legends date back from 600 BCE to 5000 BCE. By the time the Roman Empire had conquered the Mediterranean area, the mythologies of these three gods were interchangeable.

The Zoroastrian Mithra was a god-man whose birth was celebrated on December 25th. He advocated peace, love and social justice. He performed miracles, cast out demons and raised the dead. The

religion included seven ceremonial sacra-
ments, one of which was baptism by water
for the remission of sins, and another of
communion of bread and wine which repre-
sented his body and blood. An inscription
to Mithra reads: *"He who will not eat of my
body and drink of my blood, so that he will
be made one with me and I with him, the
same shall not know salvation."*[46] The
mythology of the Roman god, Bacchus,
relates an identical admonition for the
attainment of health and salvation.

Dionysus and Jesus both had god as
their father and were born in cowsheds to
virgins. Their births were prophesied by
stars in the heavens. At marriage cere-
monies they both changed water into wine.
They had twelve disciples and their followers were born again to baptism. They rode
triumphantly into cities on donkeys wherein
the inhabitants waved palm leaves. They
were both hung on crosses and killed as
sacrifices for the sins of the world. After
death, they descended into hell, and on the
third day they returned to life. Their burial
caves were visited by three female follow-

ers.[47] It is not at all unreasonable to assert that the story of Jesus is a Jewish *midrash* version of the Osiris-Dionysus mythology, of which the entire Mediterranean region was awash at that time. Even Roman Catholicism eventually replaced the statue of Diana of Ephesus with the statue of the Virgin Mary and the pantheon of gods by the pantheon of patron saints.

In all seriousness and without any motive to offend, the foregoing syllogism makes a case of probability:

If it **looks like a myth, quacks like a myth, and flies like a myth** it probably is a **myth**.
The **story of Jesus** is one that **looks like a myth, quacks like a myth, and flies like a myth**.
In that case, the **story of Jesus** probably is a **myth**.

Part Two

No More Argument, Just Personal Agnostic Just Personal Agnostic Pontification

REASON VS. FAITH

If you would be a real seeker after truth, it is necessary that at least once in your life you doubt, as far as possible, all things.
Rene Descartes

George Smith proposes that religion believers must first demonstrate that faith is capable of determining truth from fiction before they can claim that there's no conflict between reason and faith. Reason is the tool of verification. It is man's only implement for determining truth. Faith, on the contrary, is the toss of a coin, the Russian roulette of guidance to truth. Reason and faith are mutually exclusive terms. If one has arrived at the proof of a proposition by sound reasoning, it is no longer a leap of faith to believe that proposition.

"If one does not understand the concept of what god is, one does not arrive at that understanding through faith. If the doctrines of religion are absurd, they do not lose their absurdity through faith. If there are no reasons to believe in a religious doc-

trine, we do not gain reasons through faith. Faith does not erase contradictions and absurdities; it merely allows one to believe in spite of contradictions and uncertainties."[48]

CONSEQUENCES OF FAITH-BASED RELIGION

Religion is regarded by common people to be true, by the wise as false, and by the rulers as useful.
Seneca

A majority of people have jumped to the inventions of revealed religion by abandoning reason. Being forever open to suggestion and reticent to analyze, we have accepted these stories as if they were axiomatic or self-evident truths. The consequences of this abandonment of reason for revealed religion have been detrimental, not just on a holistic historical scale, but for each individual on a psycho-self-perceptual plane, and for entire cultures and communities on a psycho-social scale. We fret for sins which cannot be committed and for a damnation that does not exist. The only sins that can be committed are wrongs against real people and the environment, sins for which there are no eternal consequences.

Religious doctrines keep people apart and cause irreparable division among individuals and nations. The Israelites conquered and murdered multitudes on account of an alleged divine bequeathing of land more than 3500 years ago. They, more than any known people, have themselves been victims of prejudice, pogroms, and massacres at the hands of other faith practitioners. Christians have annihilated millions of innocent people through crusades, conquests and inquisitions in an attempt to control and disseminate their doctrine and preserve its literal meaning. Muslim extremists terrorize every part of the globe for the same reasons and suppress their own people with frightening religious strictures. The Hindu caste system and holy wars have ravaged India's so-called peaceful land.

The big picture is that the neurosis of religious faith has diminished, or at least become less neurotic, over the last three hundred years of human history. Punishment for blasphemy and inquisitions are almost a thing of the past in western civilization. The monarchies of divine right have basically ceased to exist in the west. The Catholic Church no longer professes that there is no salvation outside of its doctrinal jurisdiction. The Middle-Eastern Islamic countries are presently experiencing a state of dialectic spiritualism and groping toward civil liberties. The eventual legalization of a free press will spring them forward into an age of reason.

It is a paradox in that the various Protestant revolutions of the 15th century, based on puritanical and fundamentalist interpretations of Scripture, forced the issue of breaking down the lax monarchies of Church and State. According to Fareed Zakaria, in his book *"The Future of Freedom,"* the emerging fundamentalist sects were emboldened by the scandal of religious laxity to wrest power from the Vatican, create clergy from self-governing congregations and fight for the right of all minorities to believe and worship as they chose.[49] Thus, the fight for fundamentalism resulted in the paradox of, up to then, unknown religious and political liberty.

For all that, religious revival appears historically cyclical. Its rise has a correlation to war time and national strife. In America we seem to be in such a revival evidenced by the quantity of Christian conservatives that have been elected to office. The agendas of the multimillion dollar (tax exempt) evangelical institutions to stack legislative positions with conservative religionists are bearing fruit. Television evangelist$ such as Pat Robertson and Jerry Falwell have amassed enough wealth and political clout to create graduate learning institutions and law schools in order to perpetuate the mind-set of a democratic theocracy. The Mid-East is advancing to free thought and Americans are retreating. Personal freedom and civil liberties will suffer in the United Sates if logical people don't meet this trend with at least equal political resistence.

FUNDA-MENTAL-ISM

Violent fundamentalism, for the most part, has "evolved out" or dissipated from open societies. It exists today in fewer genetic lines of atavistic closed societies. The fundamentalist issue is a mental health issue. It can attach itself to any system of belief, be it political or religious. It eventually must separate itself from the mainstream because of its inability to mediate differences. In the event it exists in a country or society as the mainstream of consciousness then you have an expansion block or an era equivalent to a "dark age." It is the arrested development of the infantile inability to sense grey areas or issues of relativity. Fundamentalism is the adult neurosis of compulsive behavior combined with the phobia of grey areas, loose ends or relative points of view. It is the view of a world in which only absolutes exist. It is a view that is incapable of compromise or negotiation.

A fundamentalist is abnormally stressed when confronted with the insecurity of contradiction or the unknown. It is the avoidance of this painful stress which creates impulsive demands for closure on every subject. Sometimes closure, for the fundamentalist, takes its form in the elimination of opposition. He or she will take impulsive leaps of faith and hold steadfast in the face of logical opposition in lieu of existing one moment in a temporary or insecure, state of ignorance. Fundamentalists are generally followers. They crave the nostrum of leadership and authority. If they become leaders themselves, it is usually after years of tutorship and custom molding by a precursor, authority figure.

I think that it is a universal tendency to seek absolutes. Nevertheless, absolutes are a luxury that exist only in a few areas of reality. The universal set of "real things" is, by far, made up of more things that are unknown than are known. And a single incident always has several vantage points from which to solicit a cause. Well-adjusted people know that there is no alternative to living in a world with variations on one theme or an environment of multiple possi-

bilities to ultimate issues. But fundamentalists are not equipped for alternatives.

Some religious fundamentalists,
especially in the Mid-East, use the media to
disseminate their phobias and to threaten
the world outside their closed environments. These individual cells manipulate
the press and television news in order to
appear more numerous than they are.
They use the modern media to export their
issues to the outside world but not to import
the open expression of ideas into their own
enclosures. They fully realize that the dilution of their captive culture would be the
end of their control. Unfortunately, within
the Islamic world, fundamentalists continue
to be successful in recruiting other like
minds to help their cause of inflicting indis-
criminate violence against those who don't
think like they do.

I hope that rational legislation and
information reaches their enslaved societies some day. The switch to rationalism
will have to come through the dissemina-
tion of ideas and not from violent outside

forces. When contrary culture and ideas are implemented by force the irrational become martyrs and more entrenched in their faith.

Fundamentalism can accompany any belief system. Even doctrinal atheism can attract the abusive literalist, evidenced by modern day Leninist communism. Agnosticism, because it is creedless and entails the rational resignation to a multitude of possibilities for ultimate issues, is least likely to be joined by the fundamentalist personality.

The "god cause" historically leads the way in violating human rights. Atheist regimes are a modern phenomena and have exhibited the same abusive tendencies when controlled by fundamentalist personalities. But the weight of evidence for abuse in theocratic regimes stands out with far more historical significance. Even a democracy can become a fascist or a theocratic regime if the rights of minorities and freedom of speech are not constitutional guarantees. Within America some political groups have an agenda to blur the line between the separation of church and state. This fundamentalist tendency has reached the highest levels of government and is trying to entrench itself. A correlation exists in that the more a country is controlled by religion, the presence of freedom, outside exposure, education and dispersed wealth are in remission. Almost all institutional religions have fundamentalist followers that make no secret of their endeavors to realize a theocratic form of government. The common thread of any "infallible" doctrine is that it will justify the fundamentalist in building the bomb, bending the knee and shutting the eyes to the reality of the consequences of his acts; because he does it out of a conviction and love for an ultimate issue: usually god's will. They will annihilate thousands of innocent men, women, and children in order to eradicate the mere ten whom they dislike or fear. The mainstream religionists will publicly disavow the violence done in the name of their religion by others, but privately they passively say to themselves, "It must have been the will of god because everything happens

for a reason." Nothing motivates men to kill
or to be killed like a faith-based love of god.

FREEWILL

I confess that man has a freewill, but it is to milk kine, to build houses, etc. and no further.
Martin Luther

The existence of freewill is important as to its application in religion and real life. For religion, its existence creates the mutual exclusion of the notions of omniscience and predestination. As for real life, freewill signifies the evolutionary advance from instinctual reaction to one's environment to a logical choice of alternatives. Freewill and choice are not the same thing, but they are intrinsically bound together as a function of life in intelligent creatures. Freewill is the ability to voluntarily choose a certain action from a list of alternatives. The fact that we have choices doesn't mean we necessarily choose voluntarily or "freely." An action is performed "voluntarily" in the sense that it may be chosen "free" of intrinsic or extrinsic constraint. These constraints may be internal inclinations determined by DNA or other drives and forces of which we may not even be consciously aware. They may be external persuasions such as mental or physical slavery. The reality of freewill is veiled by the lack of a measurable balance (*i.e.*, a defined beginning and end) of its utility within the mixture of another reality called determinism.

That portion of "choice" which is made freely can only be estimated. Freewill is difficult to quantify or measure because it can't be observed in the vacuum of zero instinct and zero conditioned response. Some will say that its existence cannot be scientifically debated because the notion of freewill is metaphysical, and that consequently, it can only be philosophically debated as to its existence and role in reality. The agnostic/rationalist does not confine himself or herself to either the scientific or the philosophic mode of research. Any method or position is tenable until proven untenable. I personally do not believe that choice is solely "deterministic" or exclusively "free" in nature. I prefer to disregard the adjectives of "solely" and "exclusively" and rate the exercise of freewill as a matter of degree. I speak on the premise that freewill exists to a subjective degree in every move we make. Yet the degree of its function and existence is relative to the determination that nature (instinct/genetics) or conditioning (nurture) exerts over the particular impulse to act. Psychologists and anthropologists have been saying for some time now that genetics has a big role in controlling the choices we make. Fifty percent or more of the determinants for our choices are probably the result of genetic inclinations. Things like nutrition, accidental development in upbringing, exposure to chaos and freewill account for the other portions of the choice phenomenon.[50]

Genetic determination has been measured, to a certain extent, in humans by the study of identical and fraternal twins. The University of Minnesota Center for Twin and Adoption research founded by Dr. Thomas Bouchard has documented the similarities in twins who were separated at birth and brought up in different environments. The August 1997 issue of Psychology Today, relates an instance of twin brothers who were reunited in a hotel

room and as they unpacked, observers
found that they used the same brand of
shaving lotion (Canoe), hair tonic (Vitalis),
and toothpaste (an off-the-wall brand called
"Vademecum"). They both smoked Lucky
Strikes. Later they sent each other identical birthday gifts without the prompting of
the other party.[51] This type of exact duplica-
tion is statistically rare, but other occur-
rences of similarities such as the same
choice of careers, hobbies and idiosyn-
crasies are typical among twins despite
separation at birth.

These traits are not confined to twins
alone. Adopted children united later in life
with their natural parents are frequently
surprised that they have followed a path in
life more like their genetic parents than that
of the adoptive parents who raised them.
The inference for *freewillists* is that freewill
isn't completely free but may, instead, be a
sort of subset of intent relative to or within a
larger set of genetic (instinctual) and
behavioral (nurtured) predispositions. Our
only free choice may be in the selection
between the two predispositions. This also

infers, by the way, a myriad of interesting topics that would lead away from the scope of this work. Among them are the concepts that the experiences and things which our parents learned before our conception are genetically transferred as a latent blueprint for some of our own actions. And the corollary is that we are born with some innate knowledge and instructions not learned through sense perception and inference.

My agnostic view relative to what I presently know is this: freewill is limited. It is acquired. The catalysts of freewill are knowledge and objective reasoning. If nature or nurture is adverse to the will, then it takes more freewill, prompted by knowledge and guided by reason, to overcome the bias of determinism. Freewill and objective reasoning combined set us apart from less intelligent creatures (even fellow human creatures). It is freewill to which we must aspire. Freewill increases relative to a person's knowledge of self and of his or her surroundings. It is utilized relative to one's environment and the control one has over internal or external influences.

The exercise of freewill generates stress because it is choice as opposed to inclination. I perceive freewill as a virtue or discipline which will develop and increase in application as humans evolve through their animal instincts to reproduce, feed, protect themselves and enjoy life. It is, by degree, any choice made through rationalization as opposed to irrational, deterministic, autonomic, compulsive and impulsive behavior. Freewill is the utilization of logic over potentially destructive emotions. It is the implementation of personal mores in place of social conditioning. Freewill is thoughtful planning in lieu of misguided impulsive instincts. It is, in itself, neither good nor bad, but relative. Freewill is not void of mistakes or bad results.

Western religious doctrine confuses the issue of freewill with the smoke and mirrors of an implied denial of its existence on the one hand, *"Ye have not chosen me, but I have chosen you" (John 15:16)* and the converse of a misapplied acknowledgment of its existence, on the other. Religion

needs freewill as an explanation of culpability for sinful acts. The doctrinal application
of religionist freewill is bound to the mythical battle between the powers of good and
evil. The western faith-based definition of
freewill is simplistic and objective: Freewill
is the same as choice. It is "choice" made
without outside constraint. The word "voluntary" comes to mind, but it is applied in
the context of objective exterior constraints
only, not subjective interior psychological
or genetic determinants. There are no
degrees of implementation.   It's all or
nothing. Doctrinally speaking, it is either
good or bad and never relative. However,
modern theologians are beginning to recognize the role of latent survival instincts and
mental illness in the area of involuntary
antisocial behavior among humans.
Heretofore, the only acknowledged determinism in Roman Catholic thought regard-
ing choice has been the belief in the constraint of a fallen human nature.

The Catholic Church teaches that
freewill is intrinsically tainted with an inclination toward evil.   Catholic theologians

assert that humans cannot make good choices in their natural state, because they are all born infected by the consequences of the original sin of Adam, our "first parent." They say freewill is a flat choice between good and evil, and yet we are incapable of choosing the former without god's grace. In religious theory, freewill is dangerous and a threat to god's design unless it is predestined by and through god's grace to be good . . . *"There go I, but for the grace of god."* Get it? I really don't. The concept is weird and self contradictory. Even though the good work can be done for good reasons (for the love of god) and freely, it has no value to god unless it is performed in the state of grace.   Without god's grace no freewill is good will and we are helpless in avoiding evil and incurring damnation. By this doctrine, without baptism, the cleansing of original sin, and regular trips to the confessional, good works don't matter. In addition, all people will be held accountable for their bad acts despite their alleged uncontrollable nature to sin.

Now that's not only the opposite of what freewill actually is, but it is a stressful mental state of affairs! And by means of faith-based stressors like these, religion has coerced its fair share of involuntary acts out of the freewill of many a good man and woman.

MORALITY

*No one but a fool indulges in every impulse,
but what holds a desire in check is always
some other desire.*
Bertrand Russell

*Infidelity does not consist in believing or dis-
believing, it consists in professing to believe
what one does not believe.*
Thomas Paine

We are, all of us, individually and together, egocentric systems. Nothing is more obvious, apparent and necessary to us than ourselves. In comparison, we are, each one of us, like the helio-centric solar systems throughout the universe. Everything revolves around us and our own self-images. Everything outside of ourselves takes second place; our spouses, children, friends, and even god. Everything we do, we do fundamentally for our own honor and ourselves either consciously or autonomically. It's all about us, even our search, acceptance and service to a god. We may say that we love a person or even love and serve a god, but the action is initiated by the love and service to ourselves.

All of our actions are initiated from the fundamental concept of self and/or self-image. We act only in our own best interests, if not physically at least fundamentally. This fact may not appear as reality in the visible consequences of our actions, but ego and self-perception are nevertheless the source of all our decisions and deeds. The so-called "unselfish" act is based only on appearances. The things we allow to revolve around us are collected on the basis of self-admiration. In the case of human relationships, they are made up of those people who flatter us and with whom we have developed a cohesive bond of mutual admiration, or they are made up of those whom we feel will benefit us in the end. Even our good deeds, though they may appear selfless and may even be beneficial to others to the detriment of our own physical welfare, have at their core an egocentric duty to ourselves. The cool thing about all of this is that everybody else is also their own little egocentric "solar system" meshing concurrently in our space with the same selfish intentions and survival requirements. That is where morality enters. **Morality is the technique of acknowledging the rights of all the other systems around us, whether they are living or nonliving substances, and managing them and ourselves in a manner benefiting the greater good.** It is the practice of "walking in someone else's shoes" and applying the lesson learned. This is pragmatic, advantageous and utilitarian in its effect on us as individuals and others as cohabitants in the big picture.

That being said, it is no trick to apply morality to our daily lives <u>without</u> the religious belief that god's grace and the fear of eternal punishment are the only preventives to immorality and crime. The agnostic perception of life without a god, at the level where one can verbalize a justification, is generally the result of a hard-earned, well-rounded education. (Again, to be agnostic is to be one who "does not know." It is a telling quirk of human nature that it takes an education to say, "I don't know"). To say that all agnostics are formally educated would be false. But by reason of the effort that it takes to educate and separate one's self from the faith-based masses, I would wager that the agnostic's ethical profile would be more in the class of a productive and law-abiding citizen who would not throw away his or her education by willfully creating a criminal record. Most of the immoral people I have encountered during my several careers had religious beliefs but didn't follow them.

Religious moralists will tell you that god's grace and the fear of eternal punishment are the only preventives to crime. They preach that atheists are deviant because they have no fear of eternal consequences. It is not uncommon for the religious to accuse the agnostic of being so because he or she is mad at god on account of some misdirected blame for an injustice. In the same condescending breath, they assure you that they love you even though you're an idiot, and that their church's doors are open to you. (Wouldn't it be hilarious to say, "Yes! God-dammit I'm mad because the Pope just ran off with my wife!" Stranger things have happened.)

In any event, the fact that Christians, Moslems, Jews, *et alia,* do lie, steal, rape and murder trivializes their arguments for crime control via religion. And the retort of the agnostic can be that religious doctrine promotes immorality by granting to the life-long criminal an escape to heavenly paradise for a deathbed act of repentance.

Faith practitioners cannot refrain from every "immoral" act nor keep from breaking a few laws of the land any more than anyone else can. But they do a prodigious job of hiding it. Modern media has made this such a hard fact to hide that the faithful have had to come up with a bumper sticker, *"We're not perfect, just forgiven."*

Getting back to reality, why should a person be good for the sake of eternal consequences when there can be none; at least none from the god that they have defined? As we have already induced, omnipotent gods have no needs or weaknesses. If an omnipotent god exists, then neither creation, nor the vulnerability to be offended by creation, can exist at the same time. In addition, omniscience infers pre-destination, so there can be no freewill and thus, no culpability for crimes committed. Also, the omniscient god is unable to per-form the act of judging culpability for sins because judgement requires the threefold effort of observation, comparison and eval-uation; and omniscience is mutually exclu-sive of the thinking process. What about hell? You mean the hot rocks in the center of the earth? Just think about it. . . .

True morality must be based on prag-matic principles. Agnostics and religious folk alike must eventually come to the understanding that the true road to happi-ness is based on a moral life stimulated by the present fact that the act of virtue brings immediate and obvious benefit to the entire environment surrounding the act. It is superfluous to base a good work on the presumption that god will reward it here-after. (Needless to say that most religious doctrine requires god's grace and a belief in that particular faith for good works to be of any value.) The religious faithful are superstitious and conditioned to the passivity of reliance on a god-governed world. They respond positively to the saying, "There is a reason for everything." The agnostic, inversely, lives and acts by inferences of observation and not by a blind act of faith that everything is arbitrarily governed by god's will. The exercise of reason motivates good works because it is observed to be pragmatic.

Because of science much of life has become predictable and somewhat controllable. Both biological and social disease (crime) are largely preventable through cleanliness, education and dispersed wealth. Adverse conditions are not the punishments of an angry god. They are often the effects of bad management of our own personal and social behaviors. Knowledge of how things really work is a catalyst for mankind to create better living conditions within society. All men strive for happiness. The sad fact is that poverty, ignorance and desperation can cause men to choose a mistaken path to happiness and commit crimes to obtain it. If men and women are taught the knowledge of self and the reality of life, they will have a better chance at improving themselves and their surroundings. On the other hand, the religionist's effort to be virtuous based on abstract notions of eternal reward or punishment finds him neutralized when confronted with the contradictions and necessities of reality. As a consequence, the religionist will give up fulfilling the good work based on the subjective ultimate end and regress to objective selfishness, which is his natural state. Without the management skills acquired through knowledge of self and human nature the self perceived moral religionist will commit the act most detrimental (immoral) to himself and others.

Conversely, the tried and true moral agnostics are culture and creed free. They are on a quest for knowledge and the correct lifestyle. The journey begins and ends in the school of morality. The handing down of the story of the *Ten Commandments* was, I guess, inevitable but unnecessary because the precepts, for the most part, were pragmatic and would have been carried out anyway. Morality is practical and learned like every other survival technique. It is most often painfully learned through the consequences of our own mistakes. How many times do we hear good moral advice and, yet, don't actually "learn" anything until our own abuse of the surrounding environment punishes us?

From life experience, the agnostic knows the benefit of a good deal but abhors theft because of the knowledge of the consequences of theft on the economy. He has probably felt the personal pain of loss at some point for his time and hard earned profit as a victim of theft. The agnostic knows the value of camouflage to protect himself but hates the lie because of the impairment to trust and honor that it incurs. She will defend herself or her loved one to the point of death but despises murder because it means either the useless loss of a loved one or the priceless loss of the highest form of life known to exist; that is, humankind. The agnostic, who is able, enjoys good food but tries not to overeat because of the consequences of obesity; or waste the leftovers because of the benefit of conservation and the appreciation of the otherwise starving masses. He or she enjoys a good sexual life but abstains from *ex parte* affairs by knowing the pain that they inflict on the other lover and the possible disruption in children's lives from the splitting up of families. The agnostic is mentally healthy because he promotes good and avoids evil for the useful effect it has on himself and others. She doesn't bear the contrived stress of doing good or avoiding sin because of eternal consequences that don't exist. If the agnostic loves, it is a true love based on the intellectual respect and positive definition he has for his fellow creatures and surroundings. The agnostic's love of life and creatures springs from no other motive than the affirmation of the reality that he or she observes.

FINAL ASSERTIONS

The mystery of the beginning of all things is insoluble to us; and I for one must be content to remain an agnostic.
Charles Darwin

According to the laws of physics, energy and matter are eternal. The two are intrinsically bound together and they can't be created or destroyed, only altered in form. Knock off a molecule from any basic element or add a few to create another, but you can't create or eliminate the subatomic particles. If you want to see something eternal, just open your eyes. Everything you see has always existed in one form or other and will continue to do so. We know now that the basic elements of our bodies originated with the stars. Does that support the notion of reincarnation? I don't know. I'm an agnostic. Actually, the question has validity although not in the biological "incarnate" sense. The physics of dust in the wind may determine whether I might come back as a bookend but not as a pampered cow. Perhaps, since matter can't be created or destroyed, the logical foundation for our search to define god lies in some form of pantheism. But I can't say for sure . . . I'm an agnostic. The laws of physics indicate that existence, as we know it, is present by transformation through cause and effect not by creation through omnipotence. Granted.

But what about life? What is this elusive thing "life," that exists with attributes ranging from simple autonomic cell division to self awareness and arbitrary freewill in highly developed creatures? "I think therefore I am," said the self-conscious Descartes. The mystery of the existence of self awareness is the reason I am an inquiring agnostic and not an assertive atheist. I emphasize the mystery of self-conscious, self-aware life. If and when we can define the "what" and "why" of self awareness, the definition of *god* should follow *tout de suite.*

Reality encompasses inanimate and animate things. My own absence of belief in god is teased relentlessly by the intrinsic co-mingling of life and matter. Is life made up of mere subatomic particles or electromagnetic waves rendering it a purely material or physical object? Is life an immaterial thing or a subset of the energy included in the First Law of Thermodynamics? Is it substance or accidence? Is it the essence of a material object or does it merely adhere to it? I don't know.

There are obvious properties intrinsic to life, such as self awareness, that are unlike those of mere physics. Matter is mutable but not perishable. Life, however, perishes easily. Unlike the everlasting quality of matter, nothing that "lives" will "live" forever. Life has the unique quality of being temporary. It is germinated by the joinder of seed and sperm and then eventually dies. Without any exception to man's observation, when life has gone and the physical thing to which it belonged decomposes, it never returns. It comes and goes in the material world as if to challenge it in a game of survival. Its apparent finiteness begs for an answer to its magical appearance and disappearance. Yet we know that magic does not exist.

Unlike the notion of "god," which is unobservable, life is absolutely observable, yet its essence remains as unfathomable and indefinable as god. It begs the question of origin because it doesn't fit, as far as I can perceive, within the laws of physics and the norm of indestructible transformation. We have no rational explanation for the spark of life and we abstract past its apparent end to an eternity beyond. The presence and observation of life should prompt the denying atheist toward the lookout post of lingering inquisitor.

Science can give us many of the answers as to how life exists, but it has not given us the answer to "why" it exists. Does there have to be a "why?" Will there ever be an observable and quantifying answer to the meaning of life and the existence of god? Is the compulsion, itself, to define god and ultimate issues a divine joke of genetic disposition? Is it some sort of magnetic direction finder? This compulsion is a reality that some philosophers claim to be the ontological proof of the existence of god. It's not proof. Instinctual pursuit is more likely to drive us to create and make up gods than it is to reveal or define one that may really exist.

I'm going to throw this out there just as food for thought, not as a pretense to profundity; but, are the questions, "Does god exist?" and, "What is god?" really the questions that we should be asking to better ourselves? I don't know the right questions or the answers. I am the agnostic.

In the meantime, life is the very thing and the only thing from which anyone has drawn the inference that a "supernatural" life exists. Is it correct to draw an inference of supernatural from the natural? Life is life. It is here, then gone. Does it go somewhere else? It is philosophically safe to stay here on earth. One need not infer past the material world. But is that philosophically pragmatic? Venturing out, one may surmise, as I do, that life is neither natural nor supernatural, yet, in the abstract, both. To date, this paradox has defeated the explanations and exegeses of the most brilliant atheologists and theologists. Be open to the possibility of any discovery that may bring the two concepts closer together. Conscientiously disavow anything "discovered" outside of the scientific method or sound reasoning. As far as we know, life is dependent on physical matter and exists nowhere else than the three-dimensional universe. Go beyond three dimensions in your abstractions with caution. Everyone has the ability to do so. But don't give the things that are discovered there any more weight toward the burden of proof of god's existence than they deserve. It is only the imagination. That which you will find in the metaphysical stays in the metaphysical and, in a sense, can never be brought back here for objective observation.

I am forever grateful to the great philosophers, scientists, rationalists, empiricists, documenters and historians who wrote down and disseminated what they truly perceived instead of what they were told to believe. Those navigators of free thought explored the forbidden and illegal waters of knowledge and secretly disseminated their discoveries to other inquiring minds. They risked torture and death at the hands of priests, preachers, imams, rabbis and the governments that backed them. Often by use of secret societies, they eluded the inquisitions and indexes of the Catholic Church, the moral police of Islam and the excommunication of Judaism, in order to publish their proofs against magic and myth. Even in our own day, the premises and proofs of the scientist and the philosopher reach the eyes and ears of comparatively few people.

Philosophically I am a realist as opposed to an idealist. I believe reality has an existence outside of the mind. Life is not just a dream. Even though we can be deceived by the limitations of our senses and illness, those things which we do perceive as extended bodies do indeed exist. The laws of physics and biology are real.

Our will to live and our innate struggle to survive wrestle constantly with the nemesis of death. This may explain the driving force within us to create the immortal god or gods from which our own immortality must,

of necessity, be an extension. The obvious-
ness of death is counterintuitive, so we fight
it until the day it arrives. We are open to
any suggestion which says it isn't so. We
leap in desperation toward the specious
half-truths of religious doctrines and forego
the obvious facts of reality. I think, therefore I am; I see, hear, taste, touch and draw
inferences by the highly-developed tools of
my senses and brain. That is to say, I have
verifiable knowledge of reality.

I know nothing about any dimension
outside of the natural world where some
speculate that "life" goes on for eternity. I
won't accept a "guess" for a conclusion on
the subject. Speaking for myself, I would
like to have confirmation of the existence of
a good god and a lovely eternity as much
as anybody, but I will not be dishonest to
myself and well-wish it into my life under
the pressure of any individual, social group,
culture or government. If it happens that
there is a transcendence after death, that's
absolutely fabulous. Alternatively, I don't
figure that I will be any worse for wear by
sticking to what I know. Only reality and

truth are holy. If there is such a thing as a sin, it would have to be the crass acquiescence to a myth that contradicts reason.

Leaps of faith are contrary to the faculties and reasoning abilities we possess. Guessing about reality is an action unworthy of the expectations which our fellow humans have and need in us. If man is accountable for anything, to anyone, or to any god, it could only be for actions based on knowledge and freewill. I haven't met a man that knows god yet. Come forward and define it for me! But don't be afraid to be ignorant about god. No known form of justice metes out penalty for ignorance. Only an evil and tyrannic, faith-based god would punish the ignorant. True justice pities and aids the ignorant. There is no conceivable form of justice that could expect from human beings anything but action derived from observation and reason.

I know some things; I just don't know at this stage in my life what the definition of a god could be or if a god exists. I know for a philosophical and scientific fact that the "gods" of all of the religions that I have so far encountered don't exist. The life force of creatures is a mystery. We don't know how or when life started and we are driven by survival instincts to predict that it will never end. I don't attack the concept or possibility of god's existence as much as I do man's historical definitions and exploitation of the term. Faith-based religion is mental desperation and prostration before the unknown. It is an ancestral quest for magic. It has been historically a source of control and revenue for whomever can wield its power over humanity.

I haven't the least bit of angst over my present state of mind. I get so much pleasure from exercising the ability to reason and determine truth from fiction. Humans are the elite of all living creatures. <u>Without the antidote of reason our minds are as open to suggestion as our bodies are to disease</u>. The reasoning process is not an attack on the notion of god, as religionists fear, but a search for truth and knowledge. We are information collecting machines. If a creator exists and has enhanced human beings with the use of reason for their survival, then it would not make sense to abandon or sacrifice that ability for a lower form of determination of truth based on guessing. Faith is guessing, and substituting a guess for a fact is superstition.

If a creator exists that instills reason in human beings, then this creator itself would of necessity have to be compatible with reason. The creator of reason would not grant the reward of eternal life (if such exists) to the creature that gambled the use of reason away for chance. Heaven, if dependent on just desserts, could not be the award for blind credulity and a gamble that what one man said, that another man said, that god said to him, is what everybody should believe. It may not be the use of reason that discovers god, but its discovery and essence won't be unreasonable. Every religious doctrine that I know so far is unreasonable. If you can prove to me that you have found a god, then I will accept your position and be your god's best follower and preacher.

I question the so called "truths" of all "revealed" religions, not just Christianity. This *Tent Revival for Agnostics* is not an infallible revelation but an imperfect treatise constructed from my personal experiences. I hope that the reader will consider it well rounded and objective enough for appreciation. There will be people who will take my words back into their boxes and analyze the contents within the context of their scriptures. Good! That they will have read this work at all is a wonderful credit to their bravery and a step toward the reasoning process. Others will read it and say to themselves that this is how they've always felt but could never put it into words.   I thank you for your company. And there are those who will refuse to read it because "they are very secure and comfortable in their faith." Let us theorize our ultimate issues and not dogmatize the unknown. If you believe that Jesus did exist, then follow this admonition: "seek and you shall find, knock and it shall be opened unto you."

THE END
(For Now)

Biographical Data of the Author:

Matthew T. Taylor, Sr., Esq., is the father of Matthew Tipton Taylor II, and the founding partner of the law firm, Taylor, Reveley and Associates. He received his undergraduate degree from Old Dominion University in Norfolk, Virginia and his graduate degree from the University of Alabama in Tuscaloosa.

In February of 1972, at age 16, he ran away from home and joined a Catholic religious cult. After a year of home sickness he hitch-hiked back to his family and enjoyed his final years as a teenager. Having had too much fun he became riddled with guilt and cut his hair returning to the religious life. For the next ten years he trained for the priesthood but became philosophically disenchanted before ordination and left the cloth in pursuit of a secular education.

His work in the field presently includes eleven years as a religious brother in the traditional sedevacantist Roman

Catholic Religious Order of the Congregation of Mary Immaculate Queen in Spokane, Washington; ten years as a police officer and detective on the City of Norfolk, Virginia Police Department; and six years as an attorney in the Old Dominion. He is well-traveled and can survive in Spanish, French, German, and Italian.

In 1998, he almost met his death in an auto accident which rendered him comatose for six weeks and resulted in the amputation of his left leg and the disability of his right arm.

He is yet an optimist. He owns a boat.

REFERENCES

Aquinas, Thomas, *Summa Theologiae*, Ave Maria Press, 1989, written in 1274.

D'holbach, The Baron, *Le Bon Sens (Good Sense)*, Kessinger Publishing, written in 1772.

Doherty, Earl, *The Jesus Puzzle*, Canadian Humanist Publications, 1999.

Freke and Gandy, *The Jesus Mysteries*, Three Rivers Press, 1999.

Holy Bible, New International Version, International Bible Society, 1984.

Ingersoll, Robert, *The Works of Robert Ingersoll*, Dresden Edition, C.P. Farrell, 1900.

Jesseph and Craig, *Jesseph-Craig Debate*, Internet Infidels, 1997.

Kant, Immanuel, *Critique of Pure Reason*, Prometheus Books, 1990, written in 1781.

McDowell, Josh, *Evidence that Demands a Verdict*, Campus Crusade For Christ, Inc.,1979.

Mead, Frank S., *The Encyclopedia of Religious Quotations*, Fleming H. Revell Co., 1965.

Neimark, Jill, **Psychology Today**, *Nature's Clones Research on Twins*, August 1997, Cover Story.

Pagels, Elaine, *The Gnostic Gospels*, Vintage Books, 1989.

Paine, Thomas, *Age of Reason*, Dover Publications, Inc., 2004, written in 1794.

Popkin and Stroll, *Philosophy Made Simple*, Second Edition, Revised, Broadway Books, 2001.

Smith, George H., *Atheism The Case Against God*, Prometheus Books, 1989.

Still, James, *The Gospel of John and the Hellenization of Jesus*, Internet Infidels, 1995-2005.

West, E.W., Translator, *The Sacred Books of the East, The Zend Avesta*, Oxford University Press, 1897.

Zakaria, Fareed, *The Future of Freedom*, W.W. Norton and Company, 2004.

NOTES

1. Ingersoll, R., *Why I Am Agnostic*, (1900), 1
2. Popkin and Stroll, (2001), 241-252
3. Jesseph and Craig, (1997), 2
4. Aquinas, (1989), 154
5. Kant, (1990), 259
6. Smith, George H., (1989), 50
7. Ibid., 52
8. Ibid., 72
9. Ibid., 40
10. Ibid., 72
11. Ibid., 74
12. Ibid., 73
13. Ibid., 73
14. Ibid., 73
15. Ibid., 77
16. Ibid., 77
17. Ibid., 77
18. Ibid., 80
19. West, E.W., (1897), Volume Five, Verse 28
20. Paine, Thomas, (2004), 118
21. Ibid., 120
22. Ibid., 126
23. Freke and Gandy, (1999), 151
24. Based on the convincing proof found in Freke and Gandy's, *The Jesus Mysteries*, (1999)

25. Freke and Gandy, (1999), 155
26. Ibid., 155
27. Ibid., 146
28. Ibid., 147
29. Ibid., 292. This is taken from a cite used by Freke and Gandy. That reference is: *Gospel Truth* by G. Stanton, HarperCollins, 1995, p.102
30. Doherty, (1999), 81
31. Pagels, Elaine, (1989), xiii
32. Freke and Gandy, (1999), 145
33. Ibid., 145
34. Paine, Thomas, (2004), 154
35. The entire paragraph is paraphrased from: Paine, Thomas, (2004), 161-163
36. Freke and Gandy, (1999), 144
37. McDowell, Josh, (1979), 81
38. Freke and Gandy, (1999), 135
39. Ibid., 133
40. Ibid., 136
41. Ibid., 136
42. Ibid., 137
43. Ibid., 137
44. Still, James, (2005), 4
45. Freke and Gandy, (1999), 28
46. Ibid., 28, 33, 35, 49
47. Ibid., 60-61

48. Smith, George H., (1989), 124
49. Zakaria, (2004), 40
50. Neimark, Psychology Today, (August 1997), Cover Story
51. Ibid., Cover Story